CN00764655

MRS FITZHERBERT AND SONS

Portrait of Mrs Fitzherbert by Hoppner,
reproduced by courtesy of
The Metropolitan Museum of Art.

MRS FITZHERBERT AND SONS

Jim and Philippa Foord-Kelcey

Philippa Foord-Kelcey

The Book Guild Ltd
Sussex, England

The Book Guild Ltd
25 High Street
Lewes, Sussex

First published 1991

Set in Baskerville
Typeset by Southern Reproductions (Sussex)
East Grinstead, Sussex
Printed in Great Britain by
Antony Rowe Ltd
Chippenham, Wiltshire

British Library Cataloguing in Publication Data
Foord-Kelcey, Jim and Philippa
Mrs Fitzherbert and Sons
1. Great Britain George IV, King of Great Britain
I. Title
941.074092

ISBN 0 86332 559 9

CONTENTS

AUTHOR'S NOTE

This is the biography of the hitherto unknown married life of two famous people. Some readers will be familiar with the much-chronicled relationship between George, Prince of Wales (later George IV) and Maria Fitzherbert; none of them, however, will have any prior knowledge of this couple's other life together: the principle subject of the biography. Of necessity the two narratives are interwoven in this book, as they were in true life.

Vital information substantiating this biography is annotated, giving the sources. There is no annotation, however, for historically accepted facts, or for information passed down by word of mouth through the intervening generations of those few who have been privy to this secret and who have kept it so discreetly for so long.

Now, two centuries and seven monarchs later, the custodians of the secret feel that continued silence serves no purpose and this fascinating truth should be made public before it is lost forever.

PROLOGUE

June 1830

In a candle-lit room at Windsor Castle the body of King George IV lay in an open coffin awaiting burial. Beside him the Duke of Wellington, national hero, Prime Minister and executor of the dead monarch, stood guard over his old friend. It was his duty as First Lord of the Treasury to remain till the very last with the body of the King and to ensure that his dying wishes were fulfilled. Two particular requests were that nothing should be removed from his body after death and that he should be buried in the night-clothes in which he lay.

Left alone with the body, the Duke noticed that something was suspended from the King's neck by a much worn black ribbon. He was seized with an uncontrollable desire to see what it was, and coming nearer he drew aside the collar of the shirt and lo! upon the dead man's breast was a tiny locket containing a miniature of Mrs Fitzherbert. The Duke reverently drew the night-shirt over the jewel again, so that none might see. The motive of the King's dying request was now apparent to him, and the Duke saw that it was fulfilled. The King was buried with the miniature next to his heart.

PART ONE

1

1783-1786
Lovers' Meeting

At the end of the eighteenth century London was the centre of government, finance, transportation and enterprise for a thriving kingdom with ever-growing power and influence throughout the world. All the wealthy landowning families with huge country estates and impressive great houses had residences in this capital city which, after Paris, was the gayest city in the world. Here all society, men, women, young and old were devoted to the pursuit of pleasure.

In contrast, King George III with Queen Charlotte, who had been on the throne for twenty-five years had, by their parsimonious Court and strict lives, lost touch with society. They had nine sons and six daughters who lived at St James's Palace, Buckingham House and The Dutch House at Kew. In these palaces their family received the finest education while they spent their childhood under strict and harsh supervision as virtual prisoners and deprived of rational amusements.

The eldest son, George Augustus Frederick, Prince of Wales, responded to his education excellently, becoming accomplished in the classics, contemporary languages, history, literature, science and the arts. At the age of eighteen, when he became legally of age as heir to the throne, his father was compelled to give him a small establishment of his own and apartments in Buckingham House. He soon had a boyish love-affair with a young actress called Mary Robinson who in her memoirs applauded 'the graces of his person, the irresistible sweetness of his smile, the tenderness of his melodious yet manly voice, the polish and fascinating ingenuousness of his manners'. He had the happy faculty of seeming to be intensely interested in the person to whom he was talking, whoever that person might be, and he could talk on almost any subject. He loved outdoor exercise; he was a superb horseman, a good shot, an accomplished fencer, skilful in the noble art of self-defence and he could on occasions use his fists to good effect.

When he came of age in 1783 he was granted an income of £50,000 a year and his debts were cleared. He moved into his own establishment, Carlton House, overlooking gardens which are now part of St James's Park. What he lacked was paternal love, help and advice; his father was cold, stiff and unsympathetic, treating him as a child when he was a boy and as a boy when he was a man. He lost the companionship of his younger brother Frederick who was sent to Hanover. This vacuum was quickly filled and he took pleasure in associating with people of whom he knew his father would disapprove. In politics he became a Whig and he struck up a personal relationship with the King's hated brother, the Duke of Cumberland, who did his best to prejudice the Prince against his father who was a fervent Tory. He became acquainted with Admiral Jack Willett Payne whom he appointed as his private secretary and Comptroller of his household. Jack Payne became his advisor, trusted friend and confidant.

To London society, weary of the dullness and ugliness of early Georgian sovereigns, this young Prince, born on English soil, bred in England and speaking English with no Westphalian accent, came as a Prince Charming. His manly and handsome looks were the envy of every beaux, his smile the desire of all the belles and his bow the most princely bow of any Prince in Europe. For the first time for generations an English Prince was a gentleman and a wit. He soon became a connoisseur of female loveliness.

Mary Anne Smythe, known to history as Mrs Fitzherbert, the eldest daughter of Walter Smythe, Esq, of Brambridge near Winchester, was born in 1756. She had a sister and four brothers. Her father was a younger son of the Smythes of Acton Burnell, Shropshire. They were an old-established Roman Catholic family and had received a Baronetcy from

GEORGE, PRINCE OF WALES
From the painting by John Hoppner
By kind permission of the Trustees of the Wallace Collection.

Charles II in 1660 for their support of the Royalist cause. Known as Maria, she was educated in Paris at the English convent in the Faubourg St Antoine which, at that time, was the most select school for the daughters of English Roman Catholics. She loved France and Paris and she spoke and wrote French fluently. In her girlhood she was striking, not only for her physical beauty but for her sunny disposition and her unaffected manner which stemmed from her kind and guileless nature and her indefinable charm.

Mr Errington, Maria's uncle, on her mother's side, who, after her father's death was to play such an important part in her future, lived at Red Rice near Andover in the same county. The Smythes were firmly attached to their faith and Maria grew up under the ban laid upon her religion. Roman Catholic families of that day lived very much to themselves; they were regarded with dislike and suspicion by their neighbours and were largely cut off from social intercourse. No girl was brought up in greater ignorance of the world than Maria, nor led a more secluded life, yet, before long the fame of her beauty began to spread; she was not left long without suitors. In her eighteenth year she met Edward Weld, a Roman Catholic of Lulworth Castle. This elderly widower, forty-four years of age, straightaway fell in love with her. Her parents considered this a great match and the marriage was arranged. Tragically her husband died in the first year of their marriage after a riding accident, having made no provision for his widow. Maria was too beautiful and attractive to remain long without offers of marriage and she refused several suitors. In 1778, however, she married Thomas Fitzherbert, a Roman Catholic of Swynnerton in Staffordshire and of Norbury in Derbyshire. He was only ten years her senior; their marriage was a happy one and they lived on excellent terms with their Anglican neighbours.

The Fitzherberts came to their house in Park Street, London, every year. In 1778 the Roman Catholic Relief Act relaxed the severe Act of 1699 but left Roman Catholics under many disabilities. It also stirred up 'No Popery' bigotry which resulted in the Gordon riots. Roman Catholic laity worked hard to quell the tumult and protect the priests; no one was more active than Thomas Fitzherbert whose untiring labours proved fatal to him. He contracted an infection of the lungs which defied all remedies, including retreat to the warmer climate of the south of France. All efforts were in vain. Thomas Fitzherbert died at Nice on 7 May 1781 at the age of thirty-one. Maria, widowed for the second time, commissioned a memorial to him in a chapel in the town before returning to England alone. Her husband left her his London house, £2,000 a year and his horses and carriages including his phaeton with the Galloways that drew it.

Maria took a lease on the beautiful villa of Marble Hill at Twickenham; here she lived quietly for a while seeing only members of her family and intimate friends but, in March 1784, she arrived in London for the season. Lady Sefton, who was connected with the Smythe family, though not a Roman Catholic, showed the warmest sympathy and friendship towards her young kinswoman and introduced her to other ladies of both faiths and on both sides of politics, including Georgiana, Duchess of Devonshire (previously Lady Georgiana Spencer of Althorp). She was an immediate success. *The Morning Herald* of 27 July 1784 reported: 'A new Constellation has lately made an appearance in the fashionable hemisphere that engages the attention of those whose hearts are susceptible to the power of beauty. The Widow of the late Mr F - h - t has in her train half our young Nobility: as the Lady has not, as yet, discovered a partiality for any of her admirers, they are all animated with hopes of success.'

Thus, at about the same time, two sparkling superstars of opposite sexes were launched into the gaiety of London society and as was inevitable the forces of mutual attraction drew them relentlessly together.

The Prince first saw her when he was riding in Hyde Park, then on the edge of London. She was driving her phaeton and pair, wearing her widow's veil. He spurred on his horse to see her more closely. To this she responded by urging her ponies to a faster pace. At the greater speed the wind lifted the veil from her face and freed her abundant hair to the elements. They exchanged glances and he was immediately struck by this fresh and youthful apparition with her glowing locks billowing out behind her smiling face. From that moment he determined to make her acquaintance.

The fateful occasion came when Maria and her uncle, Mr Errington, were at the opera as guests of Lady Sefton, in her private box. The Prince, who was in his own box, happened to glance in the direction of Lady Sefton's party and there to his delight was the vision he had hoped to find. He went at once to Lady Sefton's box and requested that the young lady should be presented to him. He was immediately overwhelmed by her sweet nature and charm. Compared with any woman he had previously met, this was beauty of quite another calibre.* Her golden hair was unpowdered, the warm bloom of her cheeks was unrouged, her lustrous eyes were also innocent of any art, and her sunny smile was guileless. Love was instant and irresistible; from that moment he pursued her unremittingly.

At first she accepted his homage for what it was worth and the marked attentions of the young and handsome Prince, with whom half the women in London were in love, flattered her vanity if it did not touch her heart.

He was soon to learn from her good-humoured reaction to his advances that she was determined to remain virtuous. However, the more she opposed him the more persistent were his attentions. Whatever she did, it only served to inflame his ardour. She became alarmed and strove too late to break off the acquaintance. She was a woman of high principles, of irreproachable virtue, of independent fortune and good position. It was a case of marriage or nothing at all; but since marriage was impossible, it would be better, she said, for the Prince to forget her. She refused to see him any more and gave no answer to his letters.

The Prince's passion remained unabated. He vowed that he could not and would not live without her. He turned to the threat of suicide. He wounded himself quite badly, took to his bed, and called his physicians, telling them that only if they

---

* *It is a sad loss that except for one, the portraits and drawings which survive today do not stand up to the glowing tributes which have been written by so many who knew her and extolled her exceptional beauty. There were, of course, no cameras in her youth and likeness between one portrait and another is so lacking that each belies the truth of the others.*

brought Mrs Fitzherbert to his bedside would he allow them to save his life. They went to her house with this alarming report and asked her to return with them to Carlton House. She told them that nothing would persuade her to enter Carlton House without a chaperone and the Duchess of Devonshire was eventually prevailed upon to go with her. There they found the Prince pale and still bleeding. He told her that he was determined to die unless she promised to become his wife and to allow him there and then to place a ring upon her finger. On his promise to her that he would let his physicians save his life, she acceded. Admiral Jack Payne escorted the two ladies back to Maria's house in Park Street. Shocked and bewildered, they discussed the traumatic events of the night. They all agreed that Maria should write a letter to the Prince telling him that her promise of marriage, made under such circumstances, was entirely void. She knew that his marriage to her would deprive him of his right to the Throne* and to much of his income, that his brother would succeed him as Prince of Wales and to the Duchy of Cornwall with its substantial revenues. Maria knew that the marriage would provide scant security for herself or for any children of their union and could result in their marriage being dissolved by the King. In view of her own social background she had a right to expect a secure and well-endowed future for herself and her family. She knew that the Prince could not leave the country without the King's permission, which would be denied him; Maria and her two friends saw this as her opportunity to escape. They all genuinely expected that before long, in her absence, he would become attracted to another woman and forget Maria. Jack Payne agreed to deliver Maria's letter to the Prince as soon as she had made her escape.

The next day she departed in her own carriage to Margate where trusted friends gave her sanctuary while she made hasty

---

* *The Royal Princes were subject to the Act of Settlement of 1701, which forbade a member of the Royal Family to marry a Roman Catholic, and the Royal Marriage Act of 1772 which prohibited them from marrying, under the age of twenty-five, without the monarch's consent. Contravention of either of these Acts would have denied the Prince of Wales his rights of succession to the Throne.*

preparations to remain abroad for an indefinite period. Her first destination was Aix-la-Chapelle.

The object of the Prince's passion had stepped out of his reach. His only recourse was to follow her with an endless succession of couriers bearing impassioned letters. Although she knew that it was hurtful to him to receive no replies from her, she was convinced that it would be cruel to give him the smallest trace of false encouragement. Her intention was for him to forget her as quickly as possible.

For ten months she was constantly on the move. She was astonished at the speed with which the Prince's couriers could track her down whenever she tried to elude them. From Aix-la-Chapelle she fled to the Hague, from there to Paris, from Paris to Switzerland, from there to Lorraine. She was getting tired of her self-imposed and lonely exile and at Lorraine an incident occurred which convinced her that it was impossible for this state of affairs to continue indefinitely. Despite her strict retirement she became the object of the attentions of the notorious Marquis de Bellors who offered his hand in marriage. He was one of the handsomest men in France and one of the most polished and accomplished scoundrels in Europe. The young English widow, beautiful, well-connected and well-endowed, was fair game for a needy Frenchman. She refused him in a most uncompromising manner and when, despite that, he continued to urge his suit, she left Lorraine for Paris. The Prince's spies reported this and he, not knowing of her refusal of the Marquis, was acutely worried. Through his emissaries he implored her to promise that even if she would not marry him she would never marry any other person.

Maria was becoming aware of the fact that she had escaped one danger only to encounter another and to realize that she loved the Prince; she no longer had any doubts as to the sincerity of his love for her. She began to consider coming to terms with him. Maria knew that the Prince would agree any demands she made for herself but her only concern was for the welfare of their marriage and for any children of their union. She knew that for the sake of the Prince the marriage must be secret and remain secret for the rest of his life. For the sake of Maria's deep religious convictions the marriage must be acceptable in the eyes of the Church and thus make their children legitimate. For the worldly welfare of the children,

ADMIRAL JOHN WILLETT PAYNE
By Hoppner
From the Royal Collection at Windsor Castle

financial provision must be made and held in trust solely for their upbringing and their future. She wrote a letter to Jack Payne seeking his assistance and suggesting that he should come to Paris on his master's behalf to discuss the possibilities.

The next time a courier arrived she sent her letter back with him to the Admiral and within two weeks he had arrived in Paris and returned to London again to disclose Maria's anxieties and proposals to the Prince. He explained that a wife secretly married with children who could not divulge their parentage and could not be mentioned in either of their wills would be in a very insecure position in the event of the untimely death of either parent. The Prince had to admit that he did not have sufficient funds to provide an adequate sum for this purpose, particularly when he and Jack Payne had estimated the possible size of the family. Jack knew that to be the case and offered to secure a loan. The Prince besought him to do so.

This started a succession of journeys by Jack Payne between London and Paris during which the plan slowly developed. It was decided that Jack Payne, a bachelor with no family of his own, would assume the role of guardian to the children in the eyes of the world and they would take the name 'Payne'. Furthermore, in their secret family circle the Prince would adopt the name 'Randolph* Payne Esquire' while Maria would be called 'Mrs Ann Jane Payne'. Thus the foundation of the future Payne family was laid down and from then on the plan developed to suit the changing needs.

Admiral Jack Payne, who was also MP for Huntingdonshire, had many influential relatives, including René Payne, a wealthy and important figure in the banking world. He arranged a private meeting and discussed the Prince's problem. René Payne was helpful and within a few weeks he came forward with a most useful proposal. He would set up a

---

* *RANDOLPH was the name coined in the eighteenth century from ancient roots, including the Norse variation 'Randulfu', meaning 'wolf shield'. In their secret role as parents of the 'Payne' family, the adopted name 'Randolph' was known to the select circle of confidential friends who were privy to their secret, including the Spencers. it is possible that this popularized the name Randolph.*

Trust of which he would be chairman and which would be administered by a Board of Trustees consisting of the Prince, Maria, Jack Payne and any other Trustees they decided to nominate. The Trust could draw funds from René Payne's Bank up to an agreed limit. The Prince would be a guarantor of the loan and the Trust would pay interest on the amount it borrowed. He gave Jack Payne a draft of the deeds of the proposed Trust; this set out the rules for its administration in full detail.

The draft was delivered to Maria in Paris and she was overjoyed. Jack explained that the first meeting of the Trust would take place soon after the wedding when all the Trustees would set their hand to the deeds, and the welfare of her anticipated family would be secure. All that would be necessary to repay the loan would be for the Prince to pay annual sums into the Trust fund over a period of six to eight years, which should be well within his means.

The next three months were frustrating for Maria as negotiations dragged on; she longed to return to London and start her great adventure. Jack Payne, travelling in his own carriage, did not spare himself or* his horses in his anxiety to get things settled for his master and for the lady he so admired.

By the end of November everything had been achieved except the clergyman to perform the wedding service; all Maria could do was to continue her agonizing vigil. Then at last, early in December, a forty page letter arrived by courier from the Prince and one from Jack Payne. Jack Payne's letter explained that he had paid for the release of a clergyman of the Church of England who had been imprisoned for debt. He had agreed to conduct the wedding service in exchange for his release and other preferments.

In his long letter the Prince commented on the recent train of wonderful events which had taken place to facilitate the entire arrangement of their plan. To anyone with no

---

* *A story passed down through the generations of the Payne family, no doubt embellished in the course of time, tells of the great black coach and four sweating horses, urged on by the agitated Admiral, repeatedly pounding non-stop back and forth between the two capital cities, with chamber pots rocketing out of the windows at regular intervals.*

knowledge of the secret negotiations which had taken place and the secret plan that had resulted, this would be quite incomprehensible. Many pages were devoted to reminiscing over the plans he had suggested to his father during the months of her exile; the proposals he had received from his father and those he had received from the First Minister. These latter he had rejected because they did not include his marriage to his loved one. He said that 'no man had ever loved a woman as I have and do love thee' and he enclosed a miniature portrait of his eye.

He said that his courier 'Hunter', on his return to England would await her arrival at Dover and ride back at full speed to London when he knew the expected time of her return to her Park Street house, advising her to arrive in the afternoon. He said that he would come to her house in Park Street by the back way through the stables.

Maria was well-prepared for her departure and within two days she was on her way. When she arrived at Dover having met Hunter, she sent him ahead to report her impending arrival; she hurried to London and to her house in Park Street. The Prince was overjoyed at the news. He had been invited to a dance at Sir Ralph Payne's house that night, but he immediately tendered his apologies which were readily

---

* *While observers of this drama concluded that Mrs Fitzherbert had, at long last yielded to the hunger of love, W H Wilkins, the biographer, commented in 1905: 'It will always be an enigma what induced a woman of Mrs Fitzherbert's temperament and character to yield at the last. What led this pure and proud woman with her definite ideas of right and wrong, to consent to an act which, if not wrong in itself, was at least capable of wrongful interpretation?'*

Wilkins' account of the exile period was based on a Memoir published by Charles Langdale in 1856 which was based on an account of her life dictated by Mrs Fitzherbert herself (his cousin) to his brother Lord Stourton. Wilkins suggests that 'the simplest explanation of her yielding is the truest. She yielded because she loved him.'

This book, written with hindsight knowledge of the Payne family, eliminates the enigma; it shows that, having failed to end the romance, Mrs Fitzherbert resorted to purposeful discussions while keeping her distance. Having obtained the terms she needed for the secure future of her inevitable family she let her heart, again, take charge.

accepted by his host in the circumstances.

At 6 o'clock on the evening of 15 December 1785 the Prince of Wales and Mrs Fitzherbert were secretly married[2] in her own drawing-room by the Reverend Robert Burt, a Church of England clergyman. Maria's uncle and her brother were the witnesses. (Such a ceremony would be recognized as valid by her own Church.) The Prince wrote the marriage certificate in his own handwriting and it was signed by himself, his bride and the two witnesses. They left after the ceremony for their honeymoon at Ormeley Lodge on Ham Common near Richmond.

One of the Prince's first actions after his honeymoon was to appoint Lord Hugh Seymour to his Household as 'Master of the Robes' and 'Keeper of the Privy Purse'. He had served in the Navy with Jack Payne and they were the best of friends. In these two good and honourable men he confided everything. Soon after his appointment and with the Prince and Maria's blessing Lord Hugh married Lady Horatia Waldegrave, step-daughter of the Prince's uncle, the Duke of Gloucester, and a staunch friend of Maria.[4] Their responsibilities were extended to the expected secret family and their future homes. The five men and women enjoyed complete mutual confidence and trust.

The next step was to call a meeting of the Trustees to which Lord Hugh was invited. This meeting took place early in 1786 with René Payne presiding. The Prince, Maria, Jack Payne and finally René Payne all signed the Deeds of the Trust and Lord Hugh Seymour was approved as a Trustee. The deeds provided for large sums of money to be awarded to each child on coming of age and also on the death of each parent. The Chairman explained that the Trust could now draw up to £250,000 from his bank. As the amount drawn would be subject to interest it was only to be used for essential current expenditure or sound investment. He recommended the purchase of land available in Northamptonshire, Leicestershire and Warwickshire. This would produce a good rental income which would cover the interest on the loan. As the principal was progressively repaid by the Prince, the interest

An original caricature of Mrs Fitzherbert and The Prince of Wales
by Austin
Published on May 9th 1786

would diminish while the rental income would remain substantially unchanged, resulting in a steady growth of the overall value of the fund. This policy was agreed and René Payne was authorized to acquire the properties for the Trust. Jack Payne proposed that the Trust should purchase two family homes within the next six months; one near Brighton but suitably isolated, and one near Richmond. It was agreed that he, Lord Seymour and Maria should select these properties and arrange for them to be furnished and staffed.

In London the Prince lived at Carlton House and Maria in a rented house in Pall Mall nearby. They were always to be seen together but she never stayed at Carlton House overnight and at the end of an evening he would always ask Maria, with a polite bow, 'Madam, may I be allowed the honour of seeing you home in my carriage?'

Only three months after Maria's return to England there were reports in the newspapers that Mrs Fitzherbert was 'with child'. Conjecture on how her babies would be kept from public knowledge was as imaginative as was to be expected in the circumstances. There was wide circulation for the theory that Maria would be told that her child was stillborn and it would be hurried away at birth without her seeing it then or ever again. Another theory was that Maria would willingly allow her children to be banished from her care and brought up by lowly foster parents.

The story that Maria was barren, however, was the main plank on which was based the notion that the couple could not and did not have any children. The fact that there had been a son[3] by her former marriage, a baby that died* in early infancy, became a vital secret which was so well kept that there was never any necessity for it to be denied.

---

* *Both the baby and his father died in 1781 when they and Maria were staying in the south of France for the sake of Thomas Fitzherbert's health. In a letter to her daughter, Minney Dawson-Damer, written in 1825, Maria thanked her for trying to find her former husband's memorial in Nice. It seems likely that the infant son's name and dates were on this memorial. It would not be surprising if the memorial had been removed to preserve the vital secret.*

2

1786
London

In London rumour and slander were widespread; much of it centred on the implications of Maria's Roman Catholic background. It was a 'field day' for the gossip writers and the cartoonists. It is not too much to say that the coarse and scurrilous cartoons and caricatures, which were distributed in great numbers from the shops and on the streets, on the subject of the liaison between the Prince of Wales and Mrs Fitzherbert, did more than anything to drag Maria into unwilling publicity.

The Prince did everything in his power to secure, for Maria, full respect and consideration. He made it known to all his friends and intimates that honour paid to her was honour paid to him. He made it a condition that at all private parties and entertainments which he honoured with his presence, she was to be invited too. If she were not asked he would not go. He further insisted that, in her case, ordinary rules of precedence were to be waived; she should be seated at the same table as himself. His manner towards her was exactly that with which a husband would treat an honoured wife. He took a box for her at the opera and in this box he was seen with her almost every night.

At first the great majority of Maria's friends did not know what to think or how to react to her new situation. If some sort of marriage ceremony had taken place why, they wondered, was it not admitted? The Prince could not be questioned directly on such a matter, his friends met the question with evasions or denials. Mrs Fitzherbert herself had no answer but silence. She had done nothing against her conscience, she maintained, and the rest must take its chance. The Roman Catholic Church accepted her and she openly practised her religion, taking the Sacrament; this would have been impossible unless her confessor was satisfied as to her innocence.

The Duchess of Devonshire supported her strongly; she appeared in public with Maria and she was a constant and honoured guest at Devonshire House. Lady Clermont held Maria in high esteem and always supported her. The Prince and Maria often dined at Clermont House in Berkeley Square. Lady Salisbury continued to welcome her to her house. The Dukes of Gloucester and Cumberland and their Duchesses, having full knowledge, not only of the wedding but also the plans for the secret family, remained as staunch friends of the young couple.

Supported by many of her good friends she soon succeeded in living down the greater part of the insult and opposition. This was largely due to her amiability, her unassuming conduct, her kindness of heart and the straightforwardness of her manner. It was also noted, in her favour, that the Prince had greatly improved in his habits and conversation and this could only be ascribed to the influence of a good woman. His 'white rose', he called her, because of both her pale fair loveliness and her innate purity. In all this she was fortified by the private knowledge of her respectable matrimonial state. What the Prince mostly wanted was for their private life to be left alone, so that they could enjoy their new-found happiness.

The attitude of the King and the Queen was that, if the rumours of their son's marriage were true, it was the crowning act of folly and filial disobedience. The Queen consoled herself with the knowledge that whatever had passed her son was still free, in law, to marry in due course, in the tradition of the Hanovers. It was unfortunate for the Prince that his parents' consternation about his private life came at a time when he was corresponding with his father over his financial difficulties. His building operations at Carlton House were very costly. His greatest weakness was his total carelessness over money matters, which Maria tried in vain to check. As was to be expected his father refused to help him.

The London season of 1786 was one of unusual gaiety

An oval silver wirework taper stick, the filigree pattern forming stylised Prince of Wales Feathers, at the base of which a ribbon is engraved ICH DIEN. Late 18th century. Part of a lady's dressing table set.
Property of the authors.
Photograph by Kevill Armstrong.
Caption by John Bly.

despite the depression which followed the American War. Only the Court lamented the loss of 'My American colonies' and curtailed the already few and dull entertainments. At Carlton House, by the Prince's wish and desire, Maria played the part of hostess. To quote a contemporary writer:– 'this was the centre in which genius, taste and wit were to be found and to which elegance, beauty and refinement in the fair sex most amply resorted.'

Behind all the brilliance and extravagance of Carlton House lay the ever-growing menace of the Prince's debts. Again the Prince appealed to his father but when the list of liabilities included an item of £54,000 for jewellery, plate and furniture which was assumed to have been ordered for Mrs Fitzherbert,* the King was furious and took this as a pretext to refuse to help his son, now, or at any future time. This enraged the Prince, his reply to his father was to shut down Carlton House, except for a few private rooms for his own use. He stopped all construction work in progress, leaving the scaffolding as witness to the crisis and retired to Brighton to live as a private gentleman. Maria strengthened him in this resolve.

There were two other facts which prompted this precipitous action; one trivial, the close of the London season; the other momentous, Maria was pregnant.

---

* *The most likely explanation for this item of expenditure is that it was the hidden first payment into the Payne Family Trust Fund.*

3

1786-1790
Brighton – The Secret Family

The Prince had first stayed at Brighthelmstone (as Brighton was then called) in the summer of 1783 as guest of the Duke of Cumberland. Having come of age he was showing his independence and freedom from paternal control by visiting his uncle and aunt who were out of favour at Court. Sea bathing had been advised by his physicians as a remedy for swollen neck glands. He was so delighted with the little fishing village and its surroundings that he decided to acquire his own residence there. In 1784 he took a three year lease on Grove House belonging to Sir Percy Wyndham, brother of Lord Egremont of Petworth House, twenty-eight miles from Brighton. Sir Percy became one of his closest friends. He stayed at Grove House for ten weeks in 1784 and again in the summer of 1785 when he was brooding inconsolably over his missing lady love.

On 11 July 1786 he arrived back in Brighton in a hired post-chaise. Maria remained in London for two weeks to close down her rented house near Carlton House and to allow the Prince time to find her a similar small residence near to Grove House. She determined not to live under his roof until their marriage became openly acknowledged, which it never was. On her arrival she was welcomed with respect by the

---

* *To people used to present day conditions of instant and widespread communication of current events, aided by photography, fast travel and mass media, spurred on by universal inquisitiveness, this might seem impossible. With television in every home we see and hear Royalty and celebrities at close quarters frequently, in the course of our everyday lives;*

townsfolk and they settled down to a quiet life together. She was expecting her child in four months time.

Their country house near Brighton, Clapham House at Litlington, was ready for occupation. It was the first of several secret homes in which the Payne family would live as they grew up. Maria and the Prince, as Randolph Payne Esq. and Mrs Ann Jane Payne,* first stayed there in August 1786. The Prince had told his father that he intended to retire to the life of a country gentleman but he had not told him that he would do so on some occasions under a false name and without any title. Apart from two trusted servants from Maria's Park Street house the staff, who had been engaged locally, had never seen their new master and mistress before; they knew them only as Mr and Mrs Payne and in years to come they would never know them by any other names. The Prince and Maria stayed there for three days before returning to Brighton, which was about three hour's drive in Maria's phaeton.

Maria was ecstatically happy despite the stress of recent months and the slight anxiety for the future. She was an inherently happy person and it took a lot to dampen her natural infectious cheerfulness. The Prince was a loving and attentive husband. Although his charm and good nature were not as consistent as Maria's, she brought out the best in him and he was a most congenial companion for her. They had distanced themselves from the stress of recent events and were able to relax and enjoy their new life in the country together,

---

we can recognize them instantly, as easily as we can recognize members of our own family.

'During the life time of the Prince of Wales and Mrs Fitzherbert conditions were entirely different. There were not even black and white photographs and the only illustrations in newspapers were reproduced from pen and ink drawings; these were normally in the form of fanciful caricatures. The public seldom saw Royalty; most people never would. If they did, they would be dressed in elaborate and colourful ceremonial costume. Seen in the clothes of the ordinary man or woman in the street, they would probably pass unnoticed. Most of the residences of high-ranking people were large houses staffed by loyal servants and surrounded by walled-in gardens with gates. Transport was by private carriage from door to door. A high degree of privacy could be achieved.

BRIGHTHELMSTON
Church
NORTH STREET
WEST ST
MIDDLE
Kent Court
New Ship
Middle Street Cliff
Ship Street Cliff
Black Lion Street

BRIGHTON 1779

excited at the prospect of parenthood. They were both hardened travellers and continued to make frequent journeys, including visits to Maria's family in Hampshire.

In September the time had come for Maria to retire from public view. It was the end of the Brighton season and they announced their impending departure. Everyone expected that they were returning to London. The townsfolk noted that the Prince had become a reformed character; under the influence of Mrs Fitzherbert he drank less, gambled not at all, moderated his language and seemed in every way determined to lead a new life. Before they left Brighton there were further rumours that Maria was 'with child' and people were puzzled that this gossip appeared to be unfounded. The Prince and Maria had not gone to London; they returned once again to Clapham House.

The Prince divided his time between Clapham House and his private apartments in Carlton House. Days passed slowly for Maria as her time drew nearer. A few days before the baby was due her midwife arrived and a wet nurse was engaged. Maria had experienced childbirth before and was spared the fear of the unknown. If she had any worry it was for the child.

The baby was born without undue difficulty. Maria was overjoyed by this new arrival who was an enchanting little girl. Mr Payne returned very soon after the birth and stayed for several days. They named her 'Julia'. The Prince was overwhelmed with joy and was reluctant to leave his little family when the time came for him to go. As soon as she was fit to do so Maria left her little daughter in the care of her competent nurse and the housekeeper and rejoined her husband. The Secret Family had come into being and the secret Payne family home was there to stay.

Neither Mr nor Mrs Payne were away from Clapham House for long; whenever their other commitments permitted they returned to rejoin their little daughter in their private home where Mrs Payne was prepared to dwell with Mr Payne under the same roof. In the winter of 1786/7 neither the Prince nor Maria spent much time in London or Brighton. Neither had a town house, (Maria's house in Park Street was closed down) and Grove House in Brighton had been demolished in preparation for the building of the new Marine Pavilion.

Maria stayed occasionally with her friend and relative the Hon Mrs Butler and the Prince in borrowed houses at Bushey or Bagshot. They spent most of the winter at Clapham House.

Although the economies had shown some results, they had paid off the small debts and the heavy interest (9%) on the large ones, this was a drop in the ocean. The spectre of the ever-growing debts hung over them like a thunder cloud. The Prince went to his father again for help but the only result was to strain their relations yet further. He then approached his political friends who thought that the time had come to end this damaging state of affairs, but they were only a minority in the House of Commons. He tried the Government Ministers but they were afraid that if the Prince's pecuniary affairs were brought up in the House of Commons his marital status would be called into question. Frustrated, the Prince decided to get the matter raised by a private member and chose Alderman Newham. The Alderman used question time on 20 April 1787 to introduce the subject. When discussing the problems of Royalty in the House it was customary to be elusive as to the specific affairs in question and Newham referred to the Prince's 'present very embarrassing condition'. Pitt tried to nip the discussion in the bud but Newham persisted and, as feared, the 'embarrassing condition' was interpreted as the Prince's rumoured matrimonial situation. The powerful anti-Catholic country MPs then weighed in and the debate raged on, in the House, for over a week and became a bonanza for the press and cartoonists.

Eventually Charles Fox, the Prince's intimate friend, decided that the situation was becoming dangerous and that the least of the possible evils was to make an abject denial. He did so in a long winded speech which ended by claiming that 'His Royal Highness had authorized him to declare that, as a peer of Parliament he was ready in the other House to . . . afford His Majesty or His Majesty's Ministers the fullest assurance of the utter falsehood of the fact in question . . .'

The leader of the anti-Catholic group still quibbled over the matter but in due course the subject was dropped and the

House adjourned. During the debate the Prince was kept informed of all that passed and must have heard of Fox's 'denial'.

Although his principal interest was the payment of his debts he was acutely disturbed as to how Maria would take the news. He went to see her at Mrs Butler's house the day after the denial and did his best to placate her. She saw herself not only cruelly betrayed, but publicly degraded. 'This public degradation of Mrs Fitzherbert,' says Lord Stourton, 'so compromised her character and religion, and irritated her feelings, that she determined to break off all connection with the Prince, and she was only induced to receive him again into her confidence, by repeated assurances that Mr Fox had never been authorized to make the declaration; and the friends of Mrs Fitzherbert assured her, that, in this discrepancy as to the assertion of Mr Fox and the Prince, she was bound to accept the word of her husband.' Maria may not have broken off completely from the Prince but she did not forgive him easily.

The matter of the debts proceeded space. Both the King and Pitt felt that the bold stand taken by the Prince and his friends had cut the ground from under their feet. On 21 May 1787 the Prime Minister conveyed to the House the Royal message recommending a discharge of the Prince of Wales' embarrassments on the expectation that he would not contract debts in future. The House voted £161,000 in payment of the debts and £60,000 for the completion of Carlton House. The King gave the Prince another £10,000 a year out of his Civil List. The Prince was relieved and delighted but commented that 'the sum voted for Carlton House was only a third of what was necessary, and there was no grant for his new Pavilion at Brighton'. But he probably regarded the Parliamentary grant only as an instalment which would serve to tide him over his present difficulty.

The Prodigal Son was now taken back into the paternal fold and the reconciliation between father and son was made as public as their quarrel; regrettably however, in neither his financial situation, nor his relationship with the King, were these improvements to last very long.

For a time Mrs Fitzherbert would not see him and she only relented when he became quite ill from the agitation this caused him. On 25th May he took Maria to Epsom races and on their return they went to the Duchess of Gordon's Ball. Strangely, the effect of this trauma was to enhance her reputation and increase the respect in which she was held by the King's two brothers and their wives and most of the greatest ladies in society, on both sides of politics. The old Roman Catholic families rallied round her. Even the Archbishop of Canterbury noted that 'the lady is more received than she ever was, and stands more forward'.

The Prince and Maria went to Brighton early in July, where Maria received the warmest welcome. The Prince took up residence in his new Marine Pavilion and Maria at her little house near by. They were both in excellent health and buoyant spirits. The Prince indulged in healthy sports, including sea bathing every morning and cricket. Maria bathed under the protection of Martha Gunn, an old favourite of the Prince. The Prince was adored by all his retainers for his friendliness and kindly interest in their welfare.

That summer the Duke of York returned after seven years' exile in Hanover. There was a happy reunion for the Royal Family at Windsor to which the Prince of Wales had travelled all night from Brighton. The two brothers returned to Brighton where the Prince introduced the Duke of York to Maria. This started an affectionate friendship which lasted through life. Maria had given up her house in Pall Mall as an economy in 1786 but in 1788, after their finances had been temporarily improved and Carlton House was reopened, the Prince bought Maria another house in Pall Mall so that their former mode of living in London could be restored.

The King had suffered from an unfortunate recurring mental illness for many years and this condition was well-known to his family. When in his right mind, he was unusually chaste and displayed marked purity in his speech and behaviour. During his bad spells his speech, movements and eating became rapid; he was rude and used obscene language; he was irresponsible and occasionally violent. Intermittently he suffered periods of vagueness and melancholy, with moments of dreadful despair. While in this condition he was quite incapable of performing his State duties as Monarch. In 1788 the King had such a long spell of his illness that the establishment of a Regency was under active consideration.

The Prince stood by awaiting this responsibility.

However, the prospect was snatched from his grasp, by the King's sudden recovery. This had the unfortunate effect of again estranging him from his parents who regarded his as having displayed indecent eagerness for his father's decline. Had he become Regent he would have gained work and responsibilities which had been so lacking in his life, and better financial security. Instead he was left frustrated, and once again, financially embarrassed. Although the King had regular recurrences of his illness he did not require a Regent for another twenty-three years.

Early in July 1790, because they expected to be spending more time in London, the Prince and Maria decided to buy a second family home near Richmond. This was purchased from the Trust funds.[5] The new house was called Gifford Lodge and enabled them to have their little daughter nearer to them when they were in London for any length of time. That year the Prince and Maria were spending the summer in Brighton, making frequent visits to Clapham House. When the time came to return to London Maria took Julia with her and left her and her nurse at Gifford Lodge while she herself took up residence at Marble Hill, a few miles away. In August she returned to Gifford Lodge for a prolonged stay. She confided in her housekeeper that she was due to have a baby in the middle of September. Jack Payne called from time to time to discuss administrative matters. Randolph Payne Esquire arrived to see his wife quite often. Lady Horatia Seymour was a frequent visitor.

On the 17th September Mrs Payne gave birth, with the help of her midwife* and with no fuss, to a strong and healthy little boy. She employed a wet nurse as she had for Julia so that she could quickly return to her public life, without giving away to her friends and acquaintances that anything unusual had happened. A messenger was despatched to Brighton to give

---

* *Father Thurston SJ in his criticism of W H Wilkins' book* Mrs Fitzherbert and George IV *(published 1905) mentions a midwife employed by Mrs Fitzherbert.*

the glad tidings. While he was cantering through the misty valleys of the North Downs the staff at Gifford Lodge were taking their turn to congratulate Mrs Payne and to admire her new born son. Below stairs they agreed that, despite her dishevelled condition they had never seen her looking so beautiful.

Early the next day, after an overnight stay at The Kings Head at Horsham, Mr Payne arrived in his carriage and the whole household joined the proud and joyous couple in their thanksgiving and jubilations. These were slightly marred by the news of the death of the Princes' favourite uncle, the Duke of Cumberland. Both he and the Duke of Gloucester, the King's brothers, had set the example of choosing their own wives without reference to the King. They were co-conspirators with the Prince and Mrs Fitzherbert in defying the law and were privy to their secret marriage and their covert family life.

It was a month before the little boy was baptized. During this period the Prince had many engagements in London, including his uncle's funeral. It was not prudent for Maria to travel unnecessarily with her new baby. She wanted to give him her full attention for as long as possible so they did not return to Brighton for a month. When Maria set off with her two children and the nursery staff, they made a detour to Southwark. This was an insalubrious small settlement of tanneries and glue factories on the wrong side of the Thames. They stopped at St Thomas's Church where Jack Payne met them and took them all quickly into the Church where the curate was waiting near the font. The Prince and Maria's son was baptized into the Church of England and given the christian name – 'RANDOLPH'. The entry was then made into the Church Register:[6]

> October 18th 1790. Baptism of Randolph Payne.
> Son of Randolph and Ann Jane Payne.*
> Born September 17th 1790.

---

* *As Royal Families do not normally have a surname, there was no correct name for the son of a Prince of the House of Guelph to be given. The Prince of Wales had adopted the name Randolph Payne Esq for his secret life and passed on that name to the legitimate eldest son of his secret marriage.*

Jack Payne pressed five golden sovereigns into the curate's palm and the party sped on to Brighton with 'THE FIRST MR PAYNE'.

Nearly 200 years later young Randolph's bogus baptism entry was found in the Parish Records of St Thomas' Southwark. In the very comprehensive personal records which are easily available today, after a thorough search of the period before and after the event it was found that there are no records of marriages or baptisms to show that 'Randolph Payne'(the father) or 'Ann Jane Payne' (the mother) ever existed.

4

1790-1793
Sulby Hall

The bad feeling between the Prince and his parents following the King's recovery from his illness in 1789 had not been resolved. It had dragged on for over two years and threatened to bring the Monarchy into disrepute. This regrettable situation took up much of the Prince and Maria's time and attention. Many well-wishers strove to bring about a truce, including Maria herself who realized that the Prince's estrangement from the Court tended to drive him into the hands of the less desirable set of his friends. In due course these efforts by Maria and others succeeded. The King and Queen appreciated that Maria was, to some extent knowingly working against her own interests. They came to recognize her unselfish and discerning nature and gradually their prejudices against her were broken down. The Prince, on his part, was grateful to his parents for treating Maria so kindly. He was formally reconciled to the King and Queen in March 1791. Nevertheless, his new debts remained unpaid, particularly his annual repayments due to the Payne Family Trust Fund. The strain on Maria's own income was running her into debt as well.

In the spring of 1792 Mr and Mrs Payne and their family left Gifford Lodge for Clapham House and the Prince and Mrs Fitzherbert, who had run out of money, returned to Brighton to live a more economic and tranquil lifestyle. Frederick, a second son, was born to Mrs Ann Jane Payne at Clapham House. While they were there many refugees of the French Revolution came to England and a number arrived on the shore at Brighton.

In August a group of Benedictine Nuns from Montargis reached Shoreham-by-Sea in total destitution. Maria collected money for them and drove out to meet them. The party included several English men and women, a friend[7] of Maria's, Sister Catharine Dillon, and the beautiful young Duchesse de Noailles disguised as a cabin boy. The Prince paid every attention to this amiable stranger! The Prince and Maria took them all in hand personally; they gave them at first, temporary lodging in Brighton at The Ship Inn, then a furnished house in London and later they settled the Nuns in a country house at Princethorpe[11] near Rugby for a modest rent. This house was on part of the land purchased in 1786 for the Trust fund.

When settling the Benedictine Nuns at Princethorpe, they took the opportunity to stay with René Payne at Dunton Bassett in Leicestershire. He took them on a tour of some of the properties belonging to the Trust and to an estate at Sulby near Welford which belonged to his late uncle's executors. René was planning to improve this property; in 1790 he had commissioned Sir John Soane, the well-known designer of the Bank of England, to prepare[8] plans for a new house there. The Prince and Maria were very attracted both to the existing Lodge and to the planned new house. René consulted his uncle's executors who offered to rent Sulby Lodge to the Trust immediately and to sell the whole estate when a price could be agreed. This was done by putting it up for auction. René bought the property for the Trust in his own name. This expenditure on Sulby Lodge brought their loan account with René Payne's bank to its limit; they could draw no more.

Soon after their return from Northamptonshire they went into hiding and devoted themselves to family life. Only their most trusted friends knew where they were. They were thought to have been in Hampshire near Maria's family home. The Prince did rent a country house in that area, Hampshire (or Southamptonshire as it is called locally), however, they were out of the news and no one was interested in their whereabouts. In fact, they were a hundred miles away from Southamptonshire, they had gone back to *North*-amptonshire to live at Sulby Lodge! Here was a real family home where they led their lives in complete seclusion; here they experienced the freedom and pleasures of country life and hunting with one of the best packs in England, the Pytchley. They were both more than contented and the Prince kept his essential absences from his little family to the minimum.

Early in 1792 when, after the Revolution, France began her aggressive wars against Austria and Prussia, Britain at first stood aside. When, however, the French Republic encouraged revolution in other countries, executed King Louis XVI (at the beginning of 1793) and occupied Belgium, Britain started to take action. This was at first confined to an alliance with Austria, Prussia, Sardinia, Spain and Holland. Britain's policy was to subsidize her Continental allies, blockade the coasts of France and seize French colonies.

Earl Spencer, brother of the Duchess of Devonshire, Maria's friend and confidante whose family estate was at Althorp only fifteen miles from Sulby Lodge, was First Lord of the Admiralty. He needed every ship and every sailor he could lay hands on and he found that two of his most experienced senior officers, Jack Payne and Lord Hugh Seymour, had been seconded to administrative jobs in the Household of the bankrupt Prince. They both returned to active service in the Royal Navy while the Prince and his family were living in Earl Spencer's country at Sulby Lodge. The Prince's complex 'Household' with components scattered around London and Brighton, of which Jack Payne was Comptroller, had become a single country house in Northamptonshire and the 'Purse' of which Lord Seymour was 'Keeper' was empty but for bills he couldn't pay.

Back on the domestic scene a further Royal marriage took place in contravention of the Royal Marriage Act. In April 1793 the Duke of Sussex at the age of twenty married Lady Augusta Murray in Rome where he was staying for the sake of his delicate health. That autumn they returned to England and fearing that their wedding abroad might invalidate their marriage, they had a second wedding, using no titles and passing as ordinary people, at St George's Church, Hanover Square. When the King heard of the marriage of his son, despite the tears and prayers of the unhappy couple, he had no mercy; the marriage was annulled and Lady Augusta left her husband. The two children of the marriage were declared to be illegitimate.

Maria followed this tragedy with anxiety because the King's ruling against his sixth son could, at any time, be applied to the secret marriage between herself and his eldest son, the heir-apparent to the throne. Three issues were at stake: first the security of the Prince's right to the Throne (or Regency), secondly the validity of Maria's marriage and thirdly the legitimacy of her children. The present Monarch could destroy all three but, if they could keep the secret until the Prince himself became Monarch, the position of herself and her children would be unassailable.

That year their third son William was born at Sulby.

In October 1793 Sir John Soane came down to Sulby Lodge from London to show the Prince his six different proposals for improving the house;[50] the commission was still in the name of René Payne.

Engraving of Sulby Hall
Built to the design of Sir John Soane

The Prince and Maria chose a design which retained the outer shell of the house substantially unchanged but removed an adjoining complex of courtyards and single storey structures which housed the kitchen, brewhouse, laundry, dairy and coal store. The proposals replaced this with a discreet two storey servants' annexe to the house and a new stable block some distance away. The new design of the residence provided four floors, the basement floor having windows just above ground level and the top floor with dormer windows.

The house was small by Royal standards and had a modest exterior which would not display undue grandeur; the interior, however, was exquisitely appointed. The ground floor featured a large oval drawing-room and also a very spacious kitchen, pantry and larder suite, a particular partiality of the Prince. Like his exotic bedroom at Carlton House, the main bedroom had a large bow window overlooking the ornamental garden and lake. In many respects the proposed house was very similar to Maria's house near Richmond, Marble Hill. The design of the basement included separate wine, cider and beer cellars while the top floor was separated into servants' and nursery quarters, each having their own staircase. The new stable block would have a clock tower, a dairy and a laundry. Being remote from the main residence, it acted as a gate-house to protect the privacy of the family.

5

1794-1799
Three Daughters for the Prince

In due course, the Prince and Maria resumed their previous habit of wandering from home to home according to season. They also spent prolonged periods at borrowed or rented accommodation in the neighbourhood of Maria's family. The Prince's official commitments occupied much of the time and Maria also had engagements away from her family.

Their financial position was again perilous; the interest on the bank loan which created the Payne Family Trust exceeded the rental income received from the property they had purchased and, without the annual repayments by the Prince which were fundamental to the plan, this burden was increasing relentlessly. The future of the Family Trust, on which the funding of Maria's children depended, was at risk. The Prince had made repeated approaches to his parents for financial help, but his father's only thought was that the Prince of Wales should prepare himself to take over the Throne and should find himself a suitable wife who would provide him with an heir. Unless the Prince embarked on that course he would not pay one penny of his debts. That was the position which the Prince and Maria had to face. The King's terms were most disagreeable to them both. The alternative of the collapse of the Family Trust was intolerable.

When visiting his parents or attending official functions, the Prince was coming under the influence of Lady Jersey who, in contrast to Maria's call for economy, encouraged his extravagancies. Her husband, Lord Jersey, held high office in George III's Court; she herself was a favourite of Queen Charlotte who was anxious to break Mrs Fitzherbert's influence on her son. Without Jack Payne and Lord Seymour to ward off these unwelcome attentions, Lady Jersey was a formidable enemy of Maria. She was rapidly bringing the Prince under her domination. Although she was a grandmother she had irresistible fascination and charm; the Prince had no objection to her mature age; he had always preferred women older than himself. She was, however, a passionate, unprincipled and scheming person.

The Queen, observing her son's infatuation with Lady Jersey, despite her usual unswerving support for virtue, encouraged this liaison, knowing that she could bend the Prince to her will. Lady Jersey did so by repeating the current gossip that Maria cared for his rank alone and that his connection with a Roman Catholic lady was the sole cause of his unpopularity with the public. She urged that he was not bound to Maria but was free to marry anyone he wished. She secretly hoped that if she got the credit for persuading the Prince of Wales to marry a German Princess, this would advance her own interests at Court.

Under her influence these arguments, coupled with his desperate financial predicament, were too strong for him. While at Brighton he took the first step in breaking with Maria who was staying at Marble Hill, intending to join him at Brighton shortly. In the meantime they had an engagement for 23 June 1794 to meet at the Duke of Clarence's residence at Bushey near Hampton Court, for a dinner party to which they were both invited. On the morning of the dinner she received an affectionate letter from the Prince which in no way altered their planned meeting at Bushey. That night, when she arrived at the venue for the party, instead of the Prince's presence, she found an abrupt letter saying that he would never enter her house again. This was, of course, inspired by Lady Jersey.

Maria was shattered but she did not answer the letter, she disappeared and was thought to have gone abroad. She had retreated to her family at Sulby Lodge. To add to her difficulties, she was pregnant. She confided her predicament to the Benedictine Nuns at Princethorpe and they offered to give her sanctuary during her confinement. Her child was born at Princethorpe at the end of January; it was a girl. Maria decided that this little girl was hers to bring up as she wished.

She was baptized a Roman Catholic and given Maria's maiden name – Mary Anne Smythe. Maria took her relatives into her confidence and they agreed to give her all the support she needed; to the outside world this child would be regarded as Maria's niece. Maria would have liked to have formally adopted her but her public life was in tatters; instead, Mary Anne grew up with the little Paynes and, like the others, a member of the Prince and Mrs Fitzherbert's secret family.

Six weeks after dismissing Maria, the Prince had gone to his father and accepted his terms. The King was relieved that, at last, his son intended to settle down to his public responsibilities and the Prince came away from the meeting confident that the terms his father had offered would disencumber him of his debts and immediately increase his income. The King agreed to his son's plea that Mrs Fitzherbert's allowance of £3,000 per year should be continued for her life.

Encouraged by Lady Jersey, he immediately set in motion the plan for the demolition of the Marine Pavilion and Maria's small house nearby and their replacement by the Royal Pavilion to Henry Holland's design. At the same time, independent of Lady Jersey's influence, he ordered work to start on the rebuilding of Sulby Lodge to the plans agreed with Sir John Soane. This meant that very soon, Maria must give up both places for many months.

Jack Payne undertook to attend to Maria's housing problem. He disposed of Marble Hill for her and bought the house adjoining No 6, Tilney Street* which they converted into a single larger residence with a nursery suite. He found a country house called Castle Hill near to the small village of Ealing which was surrounded by pleasant country and he took out a lease on this property. With Sulby Lodge due for demolition soon, he had the Payne family moved into this new home.

---

* *Her house was near to the site where the Dorchester Hotel now stands. It has previously been referred to as Park Street.*

The King suggested two eligible German Princesses for his eldest son; one was his own niece, Caroline of Brunswick, and the other was the Queen's niece, Louise of Mecklenburg Strelitz. Louise was beautiful, talented and regal. Charles Kirkpatrick Sharpe described Caroline thus: '. . . Caroline's eyes projected . . . she made her head larger by wearing an enormous wig, she painted her eyebrows which gave her a strange and fierce look, her skin was very red, her feet and ankles were dreadful.' She was totally lacking in dignity and refinement, her conversation was broad and sometimes coarse; she was careless in her dress and not very clean. She had, however, substantial good qualities; she was warm-hearted, candid, generous and bold; she had florid good looks and a boisterous good humour. The Prince did not care which Princess he married; he is reported to have said that 'one damned frow was as good as any other'. He hoped that his break with Maria would be a temporary expedient and that, when the time came, she would meekly resume her previous relationship with him.

Lady Jersey encouraged the Prince to choose Caroline, daughter of the King's sister. The plainer the wife the better for the mistress. On 24 August 1794, cynically and recklessly, but to the delight of his father, he chose the King's niece. The King sent Lord Malmesbury to Brunswick to negotiate the marriage treaty and to bring the bride to England. Ironically, Jack Payne commanded the ship which escorted them across the North Sea. The King declared the betrothal to both Houses of Parliament on 30 December 1794.

The moment Lady Jersey knew about the marriage she gave up maligning Mrs Fitzherbert to the Prince and directed her venom against the poor young Princess. The Queen had a long-standing feud with her sister-in-law and carried this over to her daughter-in-law-to-be. She consented to Lady Jersey's appointment as Caroline's Lady-in-Waiting.

When the Princess first arrived at St James's Palace she was soon introduced to the Prince by Lord Malmesbury. She attempted to kneel to him; he raised her gracefully enough, and embraced her but said barely a word. He immediately turned away from her and slowly left the room. The astonished Princess exclaimed, '*Mon Dieu!* Is he always like that? I find him very fat and not at all like the pictures sent me.' This was followed by many more uncomplimentary remarks. A less propitious prelude to the state of Holy Matrimony would be difficult to envisage.

The wedding day arrived three days later. It started with the usual state and magnificence and with every sign of public rejoicing. On his way to the Royal Chapel the Prince said to his Chamberlain, 'It is no use, I shall never love any woman but Fitzherbert.' At the service he hardly looked at his bride and appeared more like a victim going to the scaffold than a bridegroom to the altar.

Though she did not please her husband, Caroline immediately won favour with the populace. The whole of London was illuminated and church bells rang all over the kingdom. Popular enthusiasm was great.

The objective of the Prince's marriage had been fulfilled; Princess Caroline became pregnant very promptly. Very punctually, about eight months after Mary Anne had been born to Maria, she gave birth to a daughter who was christened Charlotte and became heir-apparent to the Throne.

Lord Hugh Seymour and Lady Horatia had expressed their thorough disgust at the Prince's treatment of Maria when he first dismissed her. Lord Seymour, who had already been given temporary release by the Prince to return to active service in the Royal Navy, resigned from his office in the Prince's Household. Maria had the sympathy of all her relatives and friends including the Royal Princes, with whom she had always enjoyed a very warm and close comradeship. Furthermore, both the King and the Queen showed constant kindness to her. Maria declared, in later years, that from the moment of his son's marriage to Caroline, until his death, the King could not have acted towards her with greater tenderness and affection.

Eighteen months after the Prince had dismissed Maria he set out in earnest to retrieve her. His love for Maria returned tenfold. He dismissed Lady Jersey with considerable vehemence. He wrote his last will and testament, bequeathing all his worldly possessions to Maria, declaring that she was 'as perfectly pure as anything can be that is human and mortal' and lamenting the fact that he had been brought by base and infamous influences 'to separate from such worth'.[9] To add to his misery, he found that his debts were not paid; instead his income was increased to £125,000 per year but at the same time £73,000 was to be deducted by the Treasury each year to repay the amounts he owed.[10] This saved the Family Trust but, in the Prince's opinion, left him very poor, particularly in view of his expensive building programmes already in hand.

It was not surprising that the Prince wanted a reconciliation with Maria so that he could live with Mrs Fitzherbert, his loved one, at his exotic and luxurious new Royal Pavilion. He could not contemplate for one moment doing so with Lady Jersey or Princess Caroline. He wanted to savour these new delights with Maria and nobody else. Maria's own house near the Royal Pavilion was also ready for occupation.

Between the time of Princess Charlotte's birth and the eventual reunion of Mrs Fitzherbert with the Prince, nearly four years elapsed. During that prolonged period of time little was heard of Maria herself. To observers of the day, and as recorded in history, she was a sad childless woman deserted by her lover of the last nine years; a pathetic lonely figure who had retreated into obscurity, hoping, at least, to find peace.

But Maria was the mother of two daughters and three sons ranging from one to ten years of age, of whom the Prince was the devoted father. She was at a safe but accessible distance from the Royal residences. The Prince himself had a moral right of access to his own family; a right which Maria would not wish to deny him. He, as Mr Payne, had not been completely out of personal contact with Mrs Ann Jane Payne and their children. Towards the end of that period there had been reports of several occasions when the Prince and Mrs Fitzherbert had been seen together. Lady Jerningham wrote: 'The affair of Mrs Fitzherbert and the Prince becomes very incomprehensible; it is a fact that he meets her whenever he can, and a conversation ensues that takes them both out of the company. On Saturday, Lady Kenmare tells me, that Mrs Fitzherbert, Mrs Butler and the Prince were in a high box all night in conversation; the Princess at the Opera and also Lady Jersey. I comprehend it no longer, for I had thought Mrs Fitzherbert a woman of principle.'

In the course of these years Maria began to soften to his relentless entreaties and by 1797 they had resumed their secret rôle of loving mother and father of their young family. In addition to Castle Hill, the completely secret venues of Sulby Lodge and Clapham House were again at their disposal.

This did not entirely console the Prince, who wished passionately for a public reconciliation with Mrs Fitzherbert. Meanwhile, in popular opinion, they continued their separate existences and the Prince's craving for formal reunion was undiminished. Frustrated and angry, he threatened to proclaim their marriage. Maria, knowing that he was capable of doing any foolish thing if driven to desperation, was acutely alarmed. A public declaration of their marriage would probably have meant ruin and disgrace for the Prince and for Maria's uncle and brother who had connived at their wedding. Maria was now in the situation of having to accept any terms she was offered but nevertheless she insisted on seeking the Pope's blessing on their reunion; this could not be quickly attained. Added to that, Maria could not yet bring herself to become, in the eyes of the world, the mistress of the Princess of Wales' husband. Furthermore, during the summer of 1798, Maria had become pregnant yet again. This was not a propitious condition in which to face the glare of publicity. She also knew that if she returned to her former relationship with the Prince as Mrs Fitzherbert she would yearn to have at least one daughter with her, openly, while she was separated for any length of time from her family. That had been her plan for Mary Anne whom she had named 'Smythe', but the circumstances had foiled her. She sought the help of her trusted friend Lady Horatia Seymour who already had six children, whose husband was away at sea and who was not in good health. Maria's next child, born in November 1798 was a girl. She was baptized 'Mary Seymour' and Maria adopted her; she became the best-known of Maria's children –

'Minney'.* The Pope's approval for Maria's return to her husband was not received until late 1799.

---

* *There have been suggestions that Minney Seymour was the child of an affair between the Prince of Wales and Horatia Seymour. The Prince treated Minney as his daughter and often claimed that she was his own child. As Maria was thought to be barren it was not suspected that she was the mother.*

The relevant facts which were generally known were that Horatia was a virtuous woman and a devoted wife; she already had a large family and, furthermore, she was in a poor state of health. Both she and her husband were disgusted with the Prince for his treatment of Maria.

The facts which were not public knowledge were that Lady Horatia was a loyal friend of Maria and knew that the Prince was her husband; that Maria was not barren as was generally supposed; that the Prince and Maria already had a family; that for well over a year before Minney's birth they had been privately reunited and finally, at that time, the Prince's love for Maria was greater than ever. When the Prince claimed to be Minney's father he was telling the truth and it is a grave insult to Lady Horatia for anyone to suggest that she was the mother of a child by the Prince.

6

1797-1803
The Happiest Years

From the autumn of 1796 Admiral Jack Payne was in England with only brief spells at sea.* Maria, in particular, was relieved to have his valuable council and assistance during her troubled times and then for many of the eight years that followed; the years she described as the happiest of their married life when they were 'extremely poor but as merry as crickets.'[11] Those eight years numbered from the secret reconciliation in 1797 of Mr and Mrs Payne, not from the public reconciliation of the Prince and Mrs Fitzherbert in 1800. It will be seen from later chapters that eight years from that date extend well into an extremely miserable phase of their married life.

Late in November 1798 Jack Payne arranged the baptism of

---

* *Admiral Jack Payne had a long and distinguished career in the Royal Navy before he joined the Prince of Wales' Household. When the Prince released him and Lord Hugh Seymour from his service in 1794, at the request of Lord Spencer, Jack Payne served in the Home Fleet and Lord Hugh in the West Indies. Blockading the coasts of Napoleon occupied Europe was keeping the Home Fleet fully engaged and was proving very effective.*

Jack Payne's first appointment on returning to the Royal Navy was to HMS Russell *which was serving with the channel Fleet under Lord Howe. He took a distinguished part in the 'Glorious First of June' the naval battle in 1794 that ensured British naval supremacy against Napoleon.*

On 4 April 1795 when he returned from escorting Princess Caroline on the seven day crossing from Cuxhaven to Gravesend he was in bad

Maria's daughter as 'Mary Seymour'. He also arranged for the return of Maria's children to Sulby once the house had been rebuilt as Sulby Hall and furnished ready for occupation. He sold Maria's house at Ealing to the Duke of Kent.

Sulby Hall estate was situated in a mixture of woodland and good agricultural country, relatively flat but intersected with numerous brooks, streams and rivers in gentle sided valleys. The Hall enjoyed an isolated position one mile from the small village of Welford, which has a church dating back to the thirteenth century. A small stream which is one of the sources of the river Avon was the feature of Sulby,** where it flowed westwards along a shallow wooded valley. The house itself stood on a large terrace overlooking an ornamental lake; a most beautiful, peaceful and secluded setting.

The Payne family had their own chapel in Welford Church where they could worship in privacy when it was prudent to do so.[12] Normally, however, including Maria, they attended the services as ordinary members of the congregation, taking up most of the North aisle of the church with the complement of their indoor and outdoor staff together with their wives, children and other dependants. The estate was almost self-supporting, having its own herd of cows and a dairy, pigs and poultry. It was not only a place of beauty but also a fascinating one for children. A farm in those days was a theatre of constant cheerful activities in which all could join. The children loved to watch the cows being milked in the lofty oak beamed barn, the cream separated and the butter churned. There was excitement in collecting the eggs from around the

---

health and confined to duties ashore for eighteen months. After a further two and a half years at sea he was appointed Treasurer of Greenwich Hospital in 1799.

During those six years he was not at sea all the time and, when his ships were in port, he was able to devote himself intermittently to the Prince's service and to give Maria and her secret family such assistance as they required from time to time.

** *All that is now left of the estate are the foundations of the house overgrown with brambles and nettles, some traces of the home farm buildings, the stable and coach-house block, converted to other usage, some fine cedar, yew, oak, lime and copper beech trees, a weed-choked lake and the brick walls of a huge disused vegetable garden.*

farmyard, feeding the giant work horses in their stalls and grooming the hunters and carriage horses. The walled garden of over an acre was stocked with delicious fruit which could be picked and eaten on the spot as their successive seasons arrived: ripe strawberries, raspberries, cherries, plums, peaches, apples and pears. There was continuous activity: digging, seeding, hoeing, pruning, picking and harvesting.

The ornamental lake was a constant joy; skating in winter, fishing and boating in the summer and watching the antics of the swans and ducks as they competed for choice morsels of food thrown to them from the banks. In spring the new season emerged from the dead leaves on the ground and from the bare branches of the trees. In succession there appeared snowdrops, aconites, wild daffodils, bluebells, then the bright green leaves of beech trees, maple, oak and ash. An ever-changing kaleidoscope of colour and grace.

It was then the turn for the animal life to entertain. The cygnets and tiny ducklings were hatched and joined their parents in dignified little fleets on the water, little yellow chicks darted about the farm yard, white lambs dotted the fields, calves and foals staggered after their mothers on their precarious long legs. As Maria said in her second language, '*C'est un veritable paradis pour les enfants!*'

It was also a paradise for the grown-ups. Maria was a country woman, born and bred, and was in her element. The Prince's devotion to Maria and his children grew every day; he loved their new family home in the beautiful country setting and the seclusion ensured by the large estate. He still loved horses and hunting and, despite his somewhat excessive middle-aged weight, he was a first-class rider. He was extremely popular with all classes, country squires, farmers and labourers and enjoyed mixing with them as Mr Payne, on equal terms. His eldest daughter was a great pride to him as she blossomed into an attractive girl and made friends amongst the young people she met when cubbing and hunting.

The Prince had owned race horses since he was a young man and had training stables at Newmarket. After a visit to the races at Newmarket, he and Maria lost so much money in their betting that they could not raise £5 between them; they had not enough to pay their bill at the inn where they stayed overnight. They were deeply touched when their loyal old coachman tried to press £60 on them which, he said 'he had accumulated in the service of the best of masters and mistresses'.[11]

When the parents intended to stay in London or Brighton for any length of time they took the children with them, giving them breaks at Clapham House and Maria's new house at Parsons Green* which Jack Payne had purchased for them in 1800.

In 1799, René Payne, Chairman of the Payne Family Trust had died at the age of sixty-four. His uncle had been Governor of the Bank of England and his father had been Chairman of the East India Company. His bank was 'Smith, Payne and Smith' of Lombard Street, London and of Nottingham.**

With René Payne's death, it was essential for the Prince, Maria and Jack Payne to ensure that the Trust did not fall into disarray and that the Trusteeship had suitable continuity. Jack Payne suggested that Robert, Lord Carrington should become the new Chairman. He, formerly Robert Smith, was a partner in René Payne's Bank and guardian of his illegitimate twenty year old son George Pearce. Lord Carrington accepted but asked, in return, that his ward, George Pearce, should be appointed as Steward of the Sulby Hall estate. Maria was delighted at the proposal and the young man accepted with enthusiasm. George was the youngest of René Payne's several illegitimate children by a lady called Martha Pearce.
One of René Payne's conditions in his will was that his sons should take the name 'Payne', so George Pearce became George Payne.[13]

In June 1800, the public reconciliation† of the Prince and

---

* *East End House at Parsons Green was built in 1699 by Sir Francis Child, Lord Mayor of London and founder of Child's Bank. It was burned down in 1884.*

** *This bank later became the Union Bank of London, then the National Provincial and recently merged with the Westminster Bank to form the National Westminster Bank.*

† *Mrs Fitzherbert afterwards told Lord Stourton '. . . she hardly knew*

Mrs Fitzherbert took the form of a 'public breakfast' to meet 'His Royal Highness the Prince of Wales' at her enlarged house, 6 Tilney Street. All Maria's friends were invited and came in great numbers. The Prince let it be known that Mrs Fitzherbert should always be invited to any private entertainment which 'he honoured with his presence'.

In 1801 Lady Horatia Seymour died and only two months later her husband died at sea in the West Indies. With their death, two of Maria's friends who had given her such staunch support in her difficult years were no more. Of her original confidants only Jack Payne and her uncle Mr Errington remained.

The same year George Payne married Mary Eleanor Grey. The young couple were delighted to share a home with the Prince of Wales and fell for Maria's captivating charm. Their friendship blossomed; they enjoyed complete mutual confidence and goodwill. On 22 October 1802, Eleanor Payne gave birth to her first child, a little girl whom they called 'Mary Eleanor'. The two Payne families celebrated this happy occasion with great joy.

When Minney Seymour was four years old, members of the Seymour family started to make representations against Maria's guardianship of the child. Being staunch Anglicans, they claimed that it was unsuitable for their niece to be brought up by a Roman Catholic. Maria wished to convince them that they had nothing to fear and it did not help that she was educating Minney's nursery companion, Mary Anne, to the Roman Catholic faith. Partly for that reason and also because the Treaty of Amiens had made it possible, Maria, with the help of her friends at Princethorpe, sent Mary Anne to the convent school in Paris where she herself had been educated.

It had never been Maria's intention that her daughter should be separated from her mother and her brothers and sisters without periodical breaks at home and parental visits in

---

how she could summon up resolution to pass that severe ordeal, but thanked God she had the courage to do so'.

Paris. Unfortunately, the peace with Napoleon did not come up to expectations; soon after Mary Anne's arrival in Paris, it came to a violent end. The poor little girl was on the wrong side of the lines of battle; the conflict dragged on for years and she was separated from her family for nearly a decade.

When the Prince and Maria were in Brighton, on 18 February 1803, Sir Henry Englefield wrote of them, 'My neighbours here go on most lovingly. Their affection seems to grow with their growth and fatten with their fat'. This was not entirely due to the good living at their country seat in the shires; soon after little Mary Eleanor was born, Maria found that she herself was pregnant again and expected her next confinement to be in five months' time.

To the Prince's delight, the child, born on 3 April 1803, was a boy. He immediately offered to give him his own name, George. He soon came to be known as 'little' George Payne. It seemed an obvious course to let him be taken as Eleanor Payne's second child but only five months separated his birth from Eleanor's baby girl. Hence he was baptized when he was twelve months old, soon after Eleanor had a miscarriage. The Welford Parish Records list him as:

'George, son of George Payne Esquire and his wife Mary Eleanor.

Born 3rd April *1804*, baptized 30th April *1804*.'

This gave a seventeen month gap between the birth of the two children. He was Maria's last child.

7

1803-1811
Enter Lady Hertford

Between June 1803 and 1806 the Prince and Maria were subjected to continuous anxiety over the attempt by the Seymour family to remove Minney from Mrs Fitzherbert's custody.[15] They both resisted this strongly and in July 1803 the matter was put before the Court of Chancery where the case dragged on for many months. The Prince offered to settle £10,000 on Minney if the Seymours would consent to her remaining with Mrs Fitzherbert. In fact a greater sum had already been settled on her, under the terms of the Family Trust.

In February 1805 the Master of Chancery ruled against Maria but she was advised by her solicitor 'not to yield up the child and to appeal to the House of Lords'. Her case was duly lodged the same year. Maria sought the support of Lord Hertford, the head of the great House of Seymour. Miraculously, both Lord and Lady Hertford came over to her side in the case. When the day came for it to be argued in the House of Lords, Lord Hertford intervened at the very start of the proceedings. He said, as head of the Seymour family, that it was not right for a family matter to be debated by strangers. He put forward the proposal to their Lordships that they should make him and his wife the guardians of their 'orphaned niece', and give him a free hand in the conduct of her upbringing.

The Lords agreed unanimously and the Decree made in Chancery was reversed. Lord Hertford at once requested Mrs Fitzherbert to be the deputy guardian of 'his niece' and to continue to act as her mother. Maria and the Prince were overjoyed; after all these years of conflict with the Seymour family and their stubborn opposition, suddenly, unexpectedly and quickly their ordeal was over and everyone was on their side. Did the Seymour family come to realize that, unknowingly, they had been in the process of depriving Maria of her own daughter and of taking a young child away from her own parents? Maria retained her beloved Minney as a child whom she could treat as her own, for all to know about and to see in her company.

During the proceedings of the case in Chancery, Maria made some significant statements in written affadavits.[16] First that, early in the winter of 1802/3 she had engaged a clergyman of the Church of England to instruct Minney in the principles of that faith. This was the Reverend John Croft MA, recommended to her by the Bishop of Winchester. Secondly,[16] 'that, although she herself had been bred in the Roman Catholic faith, she always entertained and expressed the opinion that a child ought to be educated in the religion professed by its parents; and that certainly the daughter of a great family such as the Appellant, ought to be educated in the established religion of her country'.[16] Maria's children were a supreme case in point and were educated thus! She also stated 'that she had in fact educated a child (of inferior condition), born in her own house, in that religion, thinking it more advantageous for her'. This was Julia. Maria could not mention her sons nor the *most superior* (not inferior) condition of her eldest daughter Julia, the daughter of a Prince.

On 17 November 1803 Jack Payne died suddenly – a tragic loss to Maria, the Prince and their family. With his death they lost a trusted friend and ally who had masterminded and executed the plan for the welfare, funding, and security of the secret family. It was the year before Jack Payne's death that the Reverend Croft had joined them. He was a thirty-six year old bachelor and not only did he instruct Minney in reading and religion but he became the tutor and unofficial guardian of all Maria's children; he replaced Jack Payne in the select circle of confidants.

Although the eight years following Maria's secret reunion

with the Prince were the happiest of her married life, her trials and tribulations, generated by outside influences, continued to afflict her with increasing severity. It was quite tragic that Mary Anne had become marooned in Paris on the resumption of the Napoleonic Wars in 1803. Although she was known to be in good hands, her separation from the rest of the family was far longer than was intended. Apart from Mary Anne and Randolph, who were both away at school, the whole family was together most of the time. Minney stayed with 'Mrs Fitzherbert' quite often but Maria, with Minney, spent as much time as she could with the others, particularly after little George was born. The Payne family moved from house to house following the movements of their parents between Brighton, London and Northamptonshire. John Croft had apartments in each residence and moved with them. The occasions when Minney was in one house and the rest of the family in another, presented a problem to John Croft who couldn't be in both places at once. To solve this difficulty John Croft suggested to Maria that he should invite his sister to join him. Both she and Maria were delighted at the idea and Catherine Croft joined the household as her brother's assistant.

During these years there was much going on to absorb the attention of the British public besides the activities of members of the Royal family and their lady friends. They were far from being at the centre of public interest. A war was raging across the English channel and in distant oceans of the world.

Before the Treaty of Amiens, Britain's former allies on the European mainland had been overrun by Napoleon. Friends who had been on our side became allies of France and our enemies. To match Napoleon's success on land, the British had been gaining supremacy on the seas. The Battle of the Nile in 1797 had restored our Naval power at the moment when it was waning. Malta, which had been seized by Napoleon from the Knights of St John, was taken from the French by Nelson in 1800. The exiled Italian Royal family in refuge on the island of Sicily had become Nelson's friends and

Britain's protégés. The British fleet, firmly based on Malta and Sicily, had regained dominance in the Mediterranean. The Danish fleet was destroyed in 1801 at the Battle of Copenhagen.

All this exciting news, arriving in England at irregular intervals, usually many days after the events, dominated the interest of the people at home.

Further afield, Britain was free to help herself to the colonies of France and her unhappy new allies, the Spanish and the Dutch, while they were locked into a European war of expansion on land. The Cape of Good Hope and Ceylon were taken from the Dutch to secure the sea route to India. This led to the establishment by the Wellesley brothers* of British supremacy on the Indian subcontinent at the expense of the French. Less successful was the annexation of French and Spanish islands in the West Indies Archipelago and colonies on the South American mainland. However, the Navy's activities in that theatre of operation led to the interception of two French invasion fleets intending to rendezvous in the West Indies before descending on Britain. These fleets were pursued by the Royal Navy across the Atlantic and back into ports of France and Spain. No more was heard of Napoleon's invasion of England, which had been his prime objective after the Treaty of Amiens had been broken.

On the home front, joy at our successes was more conspicuous than the misery of war. British casualties were light. The progress of the industrial revolution was slightly retarded. The cost of the war was met by the introduction of a tax on income which hit the rich and the middle classes, and by higher duty on articles of consumption, resulting in higher prices which were a much more severe penalty on the poor. Amongst the middle classes some lost out through the disturbance of old established markets in Europe while others prospered through new industry in England and by exploiting the new opportunities of the expanding boundaries of overseas trade.

This period, despite the war, was notable for the prosperity of the arts, sport, literature and architecture; the country was booming.

---

* *One of whom, later, became The Duke of Wellington.*

The King's health was a matter of concern. He had recurrences of his mental illness in 1801, 1804 and 1805.

In May 1803, when the fourteen week peace came to an end and Napoleon was concentrating his forces near the Channel coast, threatening invasion, the Prince asked the Prime Minister for a Military command so that he could set an example which would 'excite the loyal energies of the nation'. One of his brothers was a Field Marshal and three were Lieutenant Generals but he, the eldest, was only Colonel of Dragoons. His request was turned down so he appealed to his father: 'I ask to be allowed to display the best energies of my character, to shed the last drop of my blood in support of your Majesty's person, crown and dignity'. The King turned down his son's request, letting him know, privately, that he expected him to stand at his side once the French invaders landed. This resulted in a quarrel between them and for eleven months they avoided each other.

The Prince and Maria's happiest hours were those which they spent at Brighton, particularly when all three of their elder sons were at boarding school nearby.* Both Maria and the Prince, as Mr and Mrs Payne, visited them often when they were in residence there but usually did so separately. They were well-practised at passing themselves off as ordinary citizens and, even at a school only a few miles from the Royal home in Brighton, they could go unrecognized when they dropped the trappings of celebrities.

After their reconciliation, Mrs Fitzherbert had not been to

---

* *At the beginning of the nineteenth century there were few public schools taking boarders. Eton, Harrow and Winchester were in existence but Lancing and Brighton College had not come into being. Many boarding schools, called academies, were private establishments belonging to the Headmaster and occupying his own property. Usually when the proprietor of such a school retired, his school closed down; thus it is not surprising that the identity of Randolph's school cannot be traced today. However, he is remembered by his descendants as saying, 'I was sent to a high-class boarding school near Brighton where I was visited often by my father, who arrived in his own coach with postillions.'*

Brighton regularly for four years. Redecoration and alterations to the Royal Pavilion had continued between 1801 and 1804, at the end of which period Mrs Fitzherbert's new house was completed, ready for her occupation; it faced the Steyne across a small garden having the entrance at the side. The chief feature from the outside was a wide covered balcony, at first floor level, which ran the full width of the house, giving an uninterrupted view to the sea. The Prince of Wales and Maria were often seen sitting on this balcony together by the hour, particularly in the mornings. Sometimes he would return greetings to an acquaintance walking on the Steyne below.

Maria's absence had been much lamented by the townsfolk and they expressed their delight at her return in 1804 by the warmth of their welcome. From that time she spent many months there every year and regarded Brighton as her home. While Brighton became a city of pleasure and glory Maria's presence, as the reigning lady, was the town's guarantee of its respectability.

In September 1805 the member of Parliament for Thetford called Thomas Creevey was staying in Brighton with his wife and daughters. He called at the Pavilion and signed the visitors' book. Creevey was a Whig and the Prince knew him as a useful needy politician whose vote was negotiable; he invited him to dinner. After dinner the Prince introduced him to Maria and requested her to call on Mrs Creevey and include her when her husband was next invited to the Pavilion. Apart from being a 'vote', the Creeveys were well-known garrulous gossips and Mrs Creevey, a superior person to her husband, was closely related to George Payne; a link with their secret home at Sulby! To preserve the family secret it was vital to cultivate the Creeveys' goodwill. Maria set about doing so in earnest; Mrs Creevey quite lost her heart to Maria.

On 6 November 1805 an exhausted messenger arrived at the Pavilion from Newhaven with an official dispatch from the Admiral of the Fleet. The message which had taken two weeks to reach England, gave the news of the glorious victory at Trafalgar together with the sad news of the death of the great national hero, Lord Nelson. Maria was the first woman in England to hear of these momentous events. The Prince was extremely affected by the death of the Admiral. He stopped all festivities at the Pavilion and by the town for ten days and then, to show his patriotism, joined with the townsfolk in celebrating the victory of Trafalgar in great style, although he did not stay for the banquet.

The 'Minney Seymour' case had been bad publicity for the Prince and Maria owing to the lingering anti-Papist feelings in the country. A row in the Royal family over the alleged bad behaviour of Princess Caroline, the deserted wife of the Prince of Wales, added to their unpopularity in the eyes of the British public. The Prince was very distressed at this because it hurt his pride.

As soon as Minney Seymour was restored legally to Mrs Fitzherbert's maternal care, she took her to Brighton for the remainder of the summer. One unfavourable outcome of the last stages of the case was that it enabled Lady Hertford to get into a close friendship with the Prince. People realized that the time when the King would either die or hand over powers to a Regent was getting closer and there was much jockeying for the corridors and boudoirs of power. Lady Hertford had her sights set on the boudoirs.

The Prince was devoted to Minney, treating her as a most cherished daughter and 1806 was a happy year for Maria, perhaps the last of the eight years she deemed to have been the happiest of their married life. Meanwhile, Lady Hertford, determined to displace Maria as the Prince's favourite, played a careful game. Throughout 1807 and 1808 she steadily pressed herself forward, trying to lure him away from Tilney Street to her own magnificent mansion in Manchester Square. In June 1807 Mrs Calvert reported on a ball at this mansion. 'Last night we went to a ball at Lady Hertford's. I think poor Mrs Fitzherbert is much deserted by him now. He has taken it into his head to fall desperately in love with Lady Hertford . . . without exception the most forbidding, haughty, unpleasant-looking woman I ever saw.'

The change in the Prince's favours was becoming more noticeable but not to Minney, who continued to refer to him as 'Prinney' and to Maria as 'Mama'. She still enjoyed parties at Tilney Street and the Royal Pavilion and the Prince was much in evidence at both venues.

The Brighton townsfolk could not imagine how so stern and unattractive a woman could influence the aging Prince. They could not have known that while he loved only Maria, he feared the hostile opinions, if not from the Brighton people, from the remainder of those who were soon to become his subjects. A bossy woman, a Protestant and a Tory suited him.

Like Lady Jersey before her, Lady Hertford knew that the weakness in the Prince's character was vanity, particularly over his yearning for popularity. This was one thing he lacked and he could not see that his own behaviour was to blame and was always seeking other explanations. That had been a secondary reason for his first break with Maria and, now he was about to become Regent, it had become an even greater obsession in the second break with the lady whom he really loved.

Emancipation of Roman Catholics and anti-Popery were the politically emotive subjects of the day. The Regent-elect felt that he must eliminate any suspicion from the minds of his subjects that any pro-Catholic sentiments lingered in his mind. His father had always been most adamantly opposed to Catholic emancipation and, when younger, the Prince of Wales had allowed it to be publicly understood that he favoured the Roman Catholic claims. This may have been dictated by three factors: his association with Mrs Fitzherbert and his desire to annoy his father, which lead to the third factor, his flirtation with the Whigs, the champions of toleration.

To emphasize openly his opposition to Catholic claims, there was no surer way than showing close intimacy with the ultra-Protestant and Tory Hertfords and his separation from Mrs Fitzherbert.

However, he was still the father of Maria's children and his paternal instincts remained strong. In 1797 he was secretly reconciled to her in his private life. Now, again, this relationship was adopted although this time, it was cool even in private. If ever they met in public they ignored each other completely. This was by mutual agreement. The Duke of

York, who was privy to their secret, acted as intermediary for their formal separation agreement. By this Maria's allowance of £3,000 per year became an annuity of £6,000. This still did not reach the full £10,000 per annum promised as her marriage settlement twenty-four years previously. To do justice to the Prince, it must be remembered that he had made secret yearly payments into the Trust fund to finance the Payne family, a fund set up for just the sort of eventuality which was now occurring. Also, by this final agreement, Maria's guardianship of their child Minney Seymour was assured.

There was no public separation and few people knew the facts. Though passion was long since dead, the Regent retained a deep feeling of respect and affection for the lady whom he knew in his heart of hearts to be his wife. So also did the poor persecuted Princess Caroline. Lady Charlotte Bury wrote, 'the Princess of Wales speaks highly of Mrs Fitzherbert. She always says, "That is the Prince's true wife. She is an excellent woman: it is a great pity he ever broke with her".' As parent of their children, he hadn't.

The happiness which Maria salvaged from her distressing matrimonial situation was attributed to Minney. Minney was outstanding for her beauty and charm of character; she had a singularly winning and affectionate disposition with a brightness and charm which attracted everyone to her. She would have been a spoilt child had not the sweetness of her nature made such a thing impossible. The truth was that as Mrs Fitzherbert's relationship with her husband was deteriorating, her other life as mother of their children had been occupying much of her time. It was also from this united family that Maria derived her continued characteristic calmness and serenity.

For the Prince and Maria, the break from a state of matrimonial contentment had not been as sudden as in 1794; it was a slow, lingering and painful process over a period of three years. But during that time Maria's life as a mother was far from empty. To the public eye she divided her time between the London and Brighton seasons, but her presence at either social scene was not continuous; both she and the Prince, together or separately, absented themselves intermittently, particularly between 1800 and 1806. Thereafter Maria was away on unrecorded activities on many occasions, some of which are described in the chapters that follow.

The Dukes of Kent and Clarence with their 'unmarried wives', were, as always the closest of friends to Maria. So also was the respectably married Duke of York, former Army Commander in Chief, who continued to live openly with Mary Anne Clarke, his mistress. This brazen lady had organized a private trade in commissions and promotions and when this had got to the knowledge of Parliament, the Duke of York had to resign as Commander in Chief. This was at a critical stage in the Peninsular war when only one month previously, the Army had lost Sir John Moore, killed at Corunna. The proceedings against his favourite son in connection with the notorious Mary Anne Clarke, culminating in his resignation, had driven the old King nearly insane but under the added distress caused by the death of his beloved daughter Amelia in November 1810, his mind gave way completely.

The Prince took the oath of Regency on 5 February 1811 at a Privy Council in Carlton House. By this achievement he had escaped the consequences of the Royal Marriage Act; so also had Maria and her secret family.

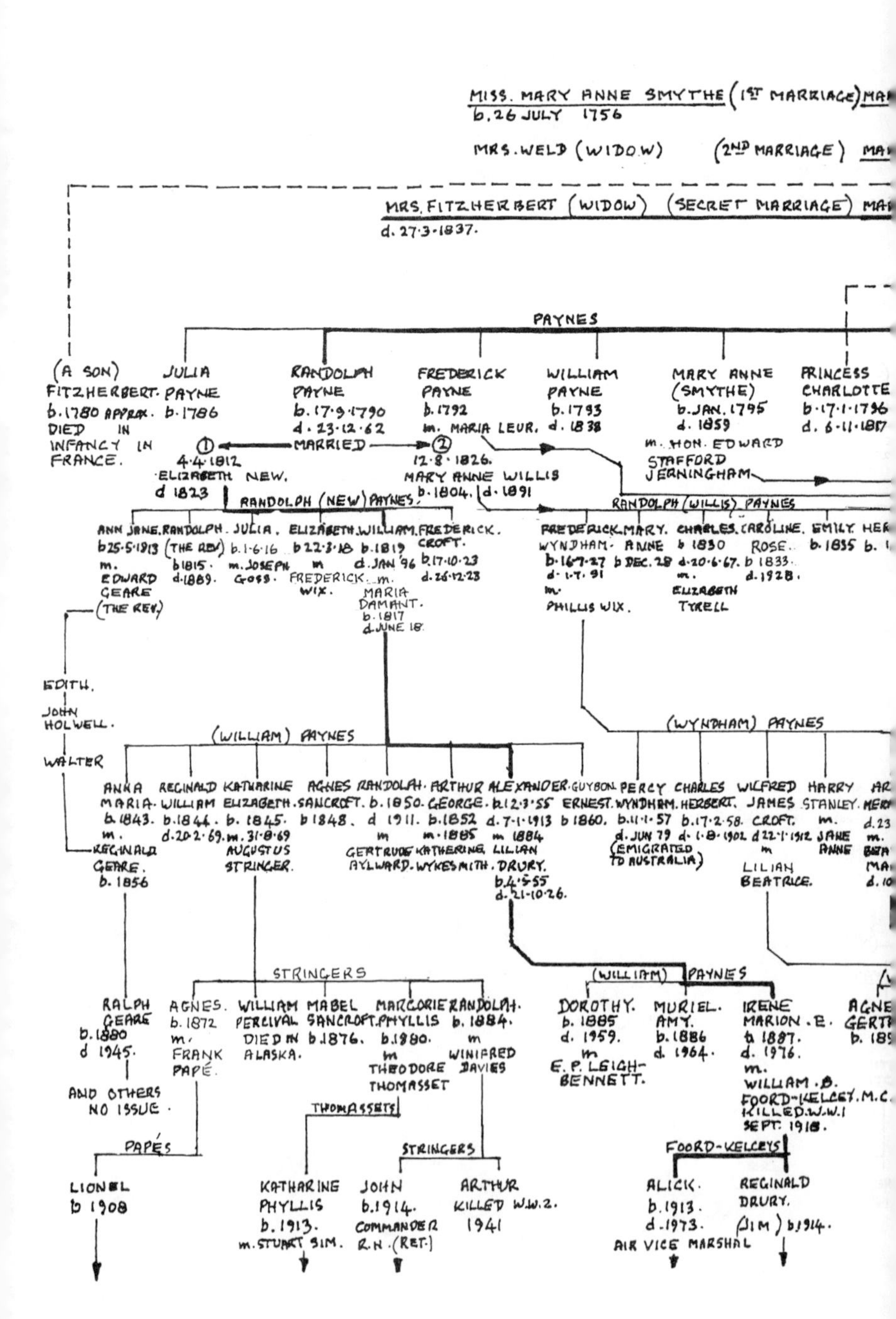
MISS. MARY ANNE SMYTHE (1ST MARRIAGE)
b. 26 JULY 1756
MRS. WELD (WIDOW) (2ND MARRIAGE)
MRS. FITZHERBERT (WIDOW) (SECRET MARRIAGE)
d. 27·3·1837.
PAYNES
(A SON) FITZHERBERT. b. 1780 APPROX. DIED IN INFANCY IN FRANCE.
JULIA PAYNE b. 1786
RANDOLPH PAYNE b. 17·9·1790 d. 23·12·62
FREDERICK PAYNE b. 1792 m. MARIA LEUR.
WILLIAM PAYNE b. 1793 d. 1838
MARY ANNE (SMYTHE) b. JAN. 1795 d. 1859 m. HON. EDWARD STAFFORD JERNINGHAM
PRINCESS CHARLOTTE b. 17·1·1796 d. 6·11·1817
① 4·4·1812 ELIZABETH NEW. d 1823
MARRIED
② 12·8·1826. MARY ANNE WILLIS b. 1804. d. 1891
RANDOLPH (NEW) PAYNES
ANN JANE. b 25·5·1813 m. EDWARD GEARE (THE REV.)
RANDOLPH (THE REV) b 1815. d. 1889.
JULIA. b. 1·6·16 m. JOSEPH GOSS.
ELIZABETH b 22·3·18 m FREDERICK WIX.
WILLIAM. b. 1819 d. JAN '96 m. MARIA DAMANT. b. 1817 d. JUNE 18
FREDERICK. CROFT. b. 17·10·23 d. 26·12·23
RANDOLPH (WILLIS) PAYNES
FREDERICK. WYNDHAM. b. 16·7·27 d. 1·7·91 m. PHILLIS WIX.
MARY ANNE b DEC. 28
CHARLES. b 1830 d. 20·6·67. m. ELIZABETH TYRELL
CAROLINE. ROSE. b 1833. d. 1928.
EMILY. b. 1835
EDITH. JOHN HOLWELL. WALTER
(WILLIAM) PAYNES
ANNA MARIA. b. 1843. m. REGINALD GEARE. b. 1856
REGINALD WILLIAM b. 1844. d. 20·2·69.
KATHARINE ELIZABETH. b. 1845. m. 31·8·69 AUGUSTUS STRINGER.
AGNES SANCROFT. b 1848.
RANDOLPH. b. 1850. d 1911. m GERTRUDE AYLWARD.
ARTHUR GEORGE. b. 1852 m. 1885 KATHERINE WYKESMITH.
ALEXANDER. b. 12·3·55 d. 7·1·1913 m 1884 LILIAN DRURY. b. 4·5·55 d. 21·10·26.
GUYBON ERNEST. b 1860.
(WYNDHAM) PAYNES
PERCY WYNDHAM. b. 11·1·57 d. JUN 79 (EMIGRATED TO AUSTRALIA)
CHARLES HERBERT. b. 17·2·58. d. 1·8·1902
WILFRED JAMES CROFT. d 22·1·1912 m LILIAN BEATRICE.
HARRY STANLEY. m. JANE ANNE
STRINGERS
RALPH GEARE b. 1880 d 1945.
AND OTHERS NO ISSUE.
AGNES. b. 1872 m. FRANK PAPÉ.
WILLIAM PERCIVAL DIED IN ALASKA.
MABEL SANCROFT. b 1876.
MARGORIE PHYLLIS b. 1880. m THEODORE THOMASSET
RANDOLPH. b. 1884. m WINIFRED DAVIES
(WILLIAM) PAYNES
DOROTHY. b. 1885 d. 1959. m E. P. LEIGH-BENNETT.
MURIEL. AMY. b. 1886 d. 1964.
IRENE MARION. E. b. 1887. d. 1976. m. WILLIAM. B. FOORD-KELCEY. M.C. KILLED W.W.1 SEPT. 1918.
THOMASSETS
PAPÉS
STRINGERS
FOORD-KELCEYS
LIONEL b 1908
KATHARINE PHYLLIS b. 1913. m. STUART SIM.
JOHN b. 1914. COMMANDER R.N. (RET.)
ARTHUR KILLED W.W.2. 1941
ALICK. b. 1913. d. 1973. AIR VICE MARSHAL
REGINALD DRURY. (JIM) b 1914.

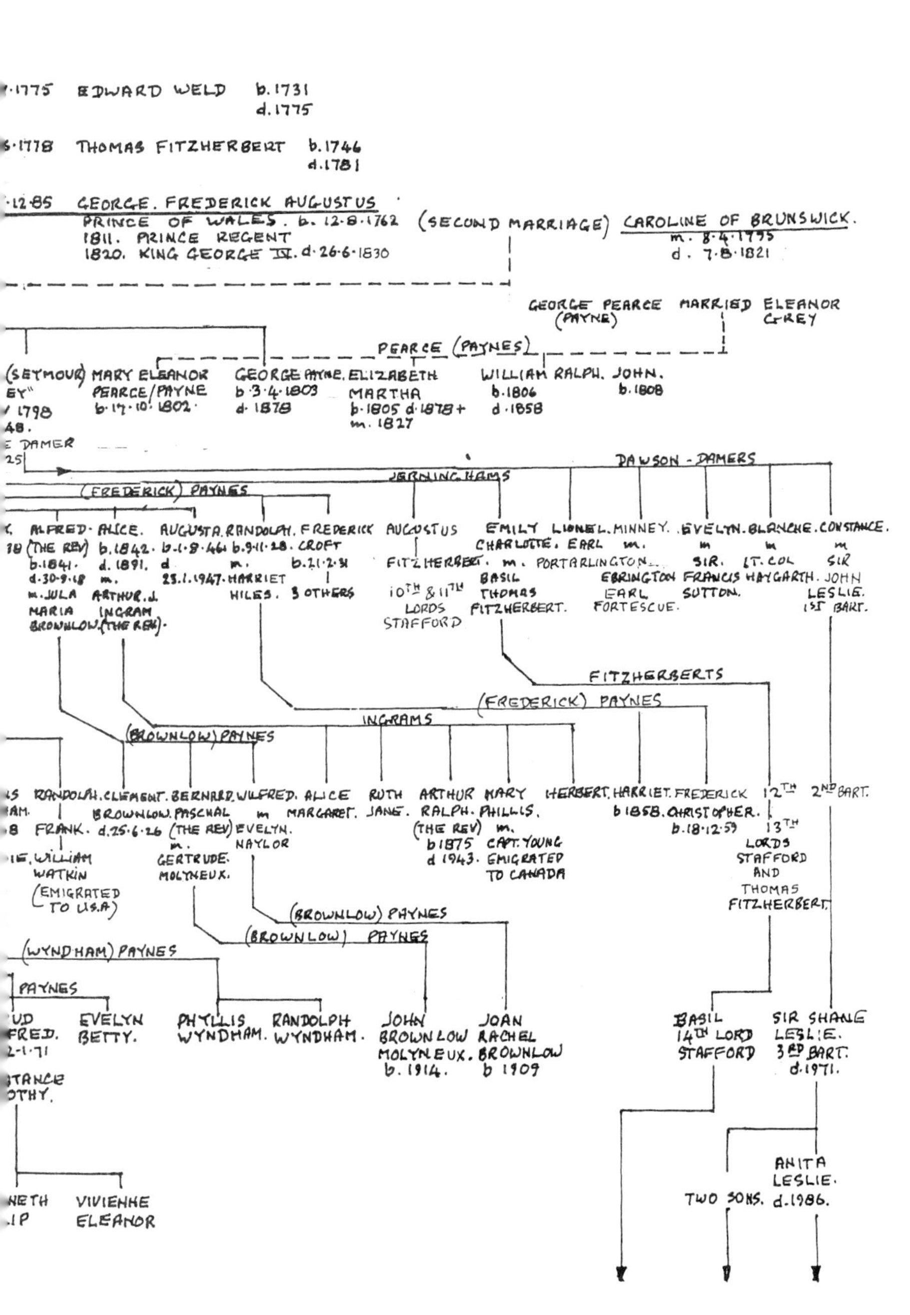

EDWARD WELD b.1731 d.1775
THOMAS FITZHERBERT b.1746 d.1781
GEORGE. FREDERICK AUGUSTUS PRINCE OF WALES. b. 12·8·1762 1811. PRINCE REGENT 1820. KING GEORGE IV. d·26·6·1830
(SECOND MARRIAGE)
CAROLINE OF BRUNSWICK. m. 8·4·1795 d. 7·8·1821
GEORGE PEARCE (PAYNE)
MARRIED
ELEANOR GREY
PEARCE (PAYNES)
MARY ELEANOR PEARCE/PAYNE b·17·10·1802
GEORGE PAYNE b 3·4·1803 d·1878
ELIZABETH MARTHA b·1805 d·1878+ m. 1827
WILLIAM RALPH. b.1806 d·1858
JOHN. b.1808
DAWSON-DAMERS
JERNINGHAMS
(FREDERICK) PAYNES
ALFRED· (THE REV) b.1841. d.30·9·18 m. JULA MARIA BROWNLOW.
ALICE. b.1842. d. 1891. m. ARTHUR J. INGRAM (THE REV).
AUGUSTA. b·1·8·46 d 23.1.1947.
RANDOLPH. b.9·11·28. m. HARRIET HILES.
FREDERICK CROFT b.21·2·31 3 OTHERS
AUGUSTUS FITZHERBERT. 10TH & 11TH LORDS STAFFORD
EMILY CHARLOTTE. m. BASIL THOMAS FITZHERBERT.
LIONEL. EARL PORTARLINGTON.
MINNEY. m. EBRINGTON EARL FORTESCUE.
EVELYN. m SIR. FRANCIS SUTTON.
BLANCHE. m LT. COL HAYGARTH.
CONSTANCE. m SIR JOHN LESLIE. 1ST BART.
FITZHERBERTS
(FREDERICK) PAYNES
INGRAMS
(BROWNLOW) PAYNES
RANDOLPH. FRANK.
CLEMENT. BROWNLOW. d.25·6·26
BERNARD. PASCHAL (THE REV) m. GERTRUDE. MOLYNEUX.
WILFRED. m EVELYN. NAYLOR
ALICE MARGARET.
RUTH JANE.
ARTHUR RALPH. (THE REV) b1875 d 1943.
MARY PHILLIS. m. CAPT. YOUNG EMIGRATED TO CANADA
HERBERT.
HARRIET. b 1858.
FREDERICK CHRISTOPHER. b.18·12·59
12TH 13TH LORDS STAFFORD AND THOMAS FITZHERBERT.
2ND BART.
WILLIAM WATKIN (EMIGRATED TO U.S.A)
(BROWNLOW) PAYNES
(BROWNLOW) PAYNES
(WYNDHAM) PAYNES
PAYNES
EVELYN BETTY.
PHYLLIS WYNDHAM.
RANDOLPH WYNDHAM.
JOHN BROWNLOW MOLYNEUX. b. 1914.
JOAN RACHEL BROWNLOW b 1909
BASIL 14TH LORD STAFFORD
SIR SHANE LESLIE. 3RD BART. d.1971.
VIVIENNE ELEANOR
TWO SONS.
ANITA LESLIE. d.1986.

PART TWO

8

1810
A Tale of the Unexpected

Five months before the Prince had become Regent there had been a serious tragedy in the Payne family. George Payne (born Pearce) was in negotiation with the Canal Company over the sale of some land just downstream of Sulby Hall where the Company wanted to build a large reservoir to supply water for the nearby stretch of their new canal. In the late summer of 1810 he was in London on this business. He was there for several weeks. It was pure chance that a certain Miss Clark of Newcastle, a close friend of George's wife Eleanor and a frequent visitor to Sulby Hall, was there at the same time in company with her brother. In due course they met at the house of a mutual friend and enjoyed each other's company. They arranged to meet again two days later, alone. Remote from the crowded domestic scene and away from the ties and conventions of a family life they found each other's company exciting. They succumbed to the excitement and they were not very discreet about it. Their conduct came to the ears of her brother who was responsible for his sister during their stay in London and who considered that George was tarnishing her honour. He remonstrated with his sister to no avail. He then confronted George who was unrelenting and resentful of this interference. After several warnings went unheeded, an unseemly crescendo of threats, insults and counter insults ensued, and Mr Clark in a fit of fury, challenged George to a duel. George's own honour was now at stake and he was impatient to end an embarrassing public scene.

He accepted the challenge.[17]

Both gentlemen appointed seconds and instructed them to meet together and proceed with the arrangements; pistols were the chosen weapons. Time and place were agreed, a pair of identical pistols was hired from a Piccadilly gunsmith. Both gentlemen went cooly about their business and pleasures for the next few days. At 5 am on 6 September, George Payne was playing cards with a group of friends in White's Club. He had been playing all night; he checked the time, rose from the table saying apologetically that he had an appointment to keep. A carriage was awaiting him at the door of the Club, he climbed in and joined his Second. They took fifty minutes to drive to Wimbledon Common and during that time darkness changed to a murky, misty dawn. They walked quickly through the trees to the appointed rendezvous where they met the Antagonist and his Second who had arrived a few moments before.

They wasted no time. Each Second gave his Principal his final instructions and his pistol, loaded and cocked. As George parted from his Second he whispered in his ear that he did not intend to return his Antagonist's fire. The two met, turned back to back. They walked away in opposite directions in time with the count-down. At 'ten' they turned to face each other and each raised his pistol and took aim. There was a single report and instantaneously George Payne toppled backwards as though he had received a heavy blow in the chest. He hit the ground and lay there, face to the sky and groaning softly. In a state of shock, as the reality of the situation struck them, they rushed to where he lay, while a round red stain expanded across his white shirt front. His Second picked up George's pistol. It had not been fired.

They carried him to one of their cabs and took him with all haste to Putney. At that hour no one was about in the village and all the houses were bolted shut. They knocked at the door of the Red Lion Inn* where eventually the landlord grumpily opened the door to send them packing but, seeing George, he beckoned them inside and he bolted the door behind them. They laid George on the floor with a pillow under his head but before they could arouse a physician, he was dead.

---

* *Legend has it that he still haunts the pub which is now called The Golden Lion.*

The survivor fled the country and George's Second wrote a letter to Eleanor giving her the dreadful news. She was left a widow with four young children and a large country estate to look after on her own. She wrote at once to Maria for help. Maria made arrangements to travel forthwith to Sulby, taking Julia, Minney, William and little George with her. One of her older servants engaged an undertaker to collect and prepare the body for delivery in a coffin to Welford Church for the funeral.

Early in the morning of 12 September, with heavy hearts, the small party set off for their long journey to Northamptonshire from Maria's new house at Parsons Green which she had purchased in 1800. They went equipped for a long stay; Maria and Minney for a few weeks but Julia,* William and Little George were to take up residence there. Randolph and Frederick were at the gate to wave the party a sad farewell. Mary Anne was still with the Blew Nuns in Paris, separated from her family by the war which still raged between England and France. When they arrived the two ladies fell into each other's arms with tears in their eyes. Eleanor's grief was greatly relieved by Maria's comforting presence.

Little George joined Eleanor's four children; Mary Eleanor, the eldest, who was nearly eight, then Elizabeth Martha who was five, William Ralph who was four and then, lastly, John, who was only three. Maria's youngest son, Little George, came between the two girls in age and they made a most friendly and lively trio when they were together, which was now to be for a long period of time.

The Gentleman's Magazine of September 1810, reporting on the duel reads: 'On Wimbledon-common, killed in a duel, Geo. Payne esq, of Sulby Abbey, near Welford, Co. Northampton. The cause of this disgraceful and fatal duel is stated in the public prints to have been an attachment to a young lady who was a visitor in the family, and sister to Mr P's

---

* *She does not feature in the archives that have been found until after Maria's death. Minney preserved two miniatures, one of a boy and one of a girl; these, she whispered, were Mrs Fitzherbert's own children. If the girl had been Marianne there would have been no need to whisper. Marianne was no secret and Minney knew that. The children must have been Randolph and his elder sister, Julia.*

antagonist. He was the younger son of the late René Payne esq. (who left him his fortune, to the amount of £14,000 a year) and nephew to Mr Creevey, MP for Thetford. He has left four children by his wife, who was Miss Gray.' The birth dates of these four children, as stated in the Welford Parish Records read:

Mary Eleanor	born 27 October 1802
Elizabeth Martha	born 29 September 1805
William Ralph	born 1 December 1806
John	born 13 March 1808

Also in the same Parish Records, as a child of the same parents, is the entry:

George	born 3 April 1804.

In all other records that survive, including that carved on the headstone of his grave, his birth date is given as 3 April 1803.

Eleanor Payne could not have given birth to George five months after her first daughter had been born. His birth date had to be falsified in the Parish Records. All five children faded from the public scene and public interest until Little George emerged from Christ Church College, Oxford, thirteen years later as a mature young man.

Before the crisis of George Payne's death, John and Catherine Croft had completed their tasks for Maria. When Maria first engaged John Croft, the Prince had promised to find him a good living when his work was completed. As Duke of Cornwall, he was patron of a number of parishes all over England and by a lucky chance one of these became vacant at the end of 1809. The Reverend John Croft MA took up this appointment early in 1810 as Rector of Berkhamsted in Hertfordshire.[33] His sister joined him there. He had become a second father to the Payne family, and both he and his sister had gained their confidence, respect and affection.

The same year Maria bought a house called Sherwood Lodge on the south bank of the Thames near the small village of Battersea with a large riverside garden. This remained a Payne family home for many years.

SUMMARY OF EVENTS CONNECTED WITH 'LITTLE' GEORGE AND SULBY HALL

René Payne, the wealthy banker from the Northamptonshire family of Paynes was born in 1735.

In 1779 René Payne's illegitimate son George Pearce was born.

Admiral John Willet Payne (Jack), the advisor and confidant of the Prince of Wales and Maria Fitzherbert, came from the Bedford branch of the Payne family. He was MP for Huntingdonshire.

René and Jack were the principal devisers and implementors of the Secret Property Trust which was set up in 1785 to finance the Prince and Maria's anticipated family.

The property Trust purchased extensive tracts of land in the shires in 1786, adding Sulby Lodge in 1792. The Prince and Maria resided there frequently.

In 1790 Sir John Soane was commissioned by René Payne to design a grander residence to replace Sulby Lodge.

In 1794 the Prince rebuilt the house to Sir John Soane's design as Sulby Hall.

From 1797 onwards the Prince and Maria made prolonged stays at Sulby Hall with their young family, assuming the name 'Payne'.

In 1799 René Payne died and his son George Pearce became the Prince's steward at Sulby Hall.

René Payne's will stipulated that all his sons should change their names from Pearce to Payne. George Pearce became George Payne.

In 1801 George Payne married Mary Eleanor Grey.

In 1802 Eleanor Payne's first child, Mary Eleanor, was born at Sulby Hall.

In 1803 Maria's last child was born at Sulby Hall and baptised at Welford Church with the name 'George Payne' in April *1804.*

In 1805, 1806 and 1808 Eleanor Payne had a second daughter, Elizabeth Martha, and two sons, William Ralph and John. In his childhood 'Little George' shared the nursery with the four Payne children during his periodical visits to Sulby Hall.

In 1810 George Payne was killed in a duel, leaving Eleanor a widow with four children.

9

1811
The Turning Point for Maria

When Parliament decided to appoint a Regent there was a Tory government under Spencer Perceval, in whom the Prince lacked confidence. The Regency Bill had, much to the humiliation of the fifty year old Prince and to the annoyance of his brothers, imposed a twelve month probationary period during which the Regent could not take measures of a lasting character. On the eve of assuming the Regency, the Prince called Maria from Brighton to Carlton House. On her arrival, to her surprise, he asked her advice as to which party he should put in office when he came to power the next day. She recommended that he should not immediately antagonize Spencer Perceval and his political party but retain them for six weeks; then, if he wished, he could find some pretext to dismiss them.

Under some obvious uneasiness he said, 'It is impossible, I have promised'.

Finding herself unable to help him in his predicament, she asked to be allowed to return to Brighton. She then offered the unsolicited advice that he should be kinder to his daughter Princess Charlotte, then fifteen years of age.

'You now, Sir, she said, 'may mould her at your pleasure, but soon it will not be so; and she may become, from mismanagement, a thorn in your side for life.'

'That is your opinion, Madam,' was his only reply.[11]

One of his first actions when he had the power to do so was to promote himself to the rank of Field Marshal and to reinstate his brother the Duke of York as Commander in Chief. He decided to inaugurate his Regency with a splendid fête at

Carlton House on 19 June, to which the French Royal family, who were living in exile at Hartwell House in Buckinghamshire, were invited as the honoured guests. The two thousand other people invited included everyone of importance, together with Maria. She discovered, however, from a well-informed quarter, that she would not be at his table, whereas Lord and Lady Hertford would be thus honoured. Courageously she sought an audience with the Regent and asked where she was to sit.

'You know, Madam, you have no place.'

'None Sir,' she replied 'but such as you choose to give me.'

With that she withdrew. Princess Caroline was not even invited to the fête.

Mrs Fitzherbert decided not to attend the fête but to go to Paris instead.

That year Napoleon embarked on his disastrous campaign against Russia. The French people were suffering widespread misery and poverty as a result of the cost and effects of his seemingly endless wars. With a 600,000 strong French army drawn from the homeland, and the fighting fifteen hundred miles away, there was a relatively peaceful situation in France. Hostility of the French people was turning away from the British towards Napoleon himself. Maria decided that the lull in the war this side of Europe gave her an opportunity to travel, in reasonable safety, to bring Mary Anne home from Paris. Both Mary Anne and Maria could speak, read and write the French language perfectly and both were Roman Catholics. They would have no more difficulty travelling the roads of France, which Maria knew so well, than any Frenchwoman. She had many friends in the capital and elsewhere who would help her out of a difficulty. She had decided to travel in June because the roads and the weather would be at their best, returning the same month. Randolph offered to accompany her as an escort; he argued that he spoke French quite well, would benefit from the practice and that he had never had a chance to go abroad before. She accepted his suggestion with enthusiasm.

Before the Napoleonic wars it was quite usual for English people of all classes to travel and live on the Continent, as Maria had done in the 1780s, not just for brief holidays but in the normal course of their lives. The number of English, counting masters and their servants, touring or resident on the Continent in 1785 was probably about 40,000, the wealthiest staying partly at inns and partly as guests in the houses of foreign nobility.

The Napoleonic wars were not total war; they were a struggle between relatively small armies and navies and the only non-combatants who were much affected were the unlucky few whose homes and lands were at the scenes of battle. They were, of course, affected economically by higher prices and taxes and by disruption of trade.

In the Spring of 1811 Maria and her family travelled to Berkhamsted to stay with John Croft at his rectory. It was a very happy reunion and the boys were fascinated by the Grand Union Canal which passed the old castle and was busy with barge traffic going in both directions laden with materials of every description in bulk, while some barges were unloading building supplies at the wharf for the great reconstruction of Ashridge House nearby.

During their stay they were entertained at a country house in the Ashridge estate by Lady Charlotte, widow of the seventh Earl of Bridgewater, who held sway on the estate at the time. She drove them to see the work in progress and then for a tour of the property, along its beautiful meandering woodland drives, down the long straight rides and on the terrace high up on the edge of the Chiltern Hills with the magnificent distant views over the Vale of Aylesbury and beyond. Back in her temporary home, having heard that Maria intended to go to France, Lady Charlotte gave her a letter of introduction to the eighth Earl of Bridgewater who, as a loyal Englishman, had lived in Paris without any attempt to disguise his true allegiance and had remained quite unaffected by the state of war with his host country.

Maria regretted that Little George would not have the benefit of John Croft's religious guidance and instruction and discussed the possibility of the boy spending regular periods of time with him until he could go to boarding school. John was very interested in the proposal and asked the whole family to treat his rectory as a second home, coming to stay whenever they chose to do so. Jack Payne having passed away and with the Prince of Wales now having the responsibilities of Regent, her children lacked the fatherly guidance which John Croft had provided for so long. No one required any persuasion. They discussed this at length and, before they left, Maria had offered John £500 towards rebuilding the rectory to the architectural style of the day and having more rooms for visitors. Little George was to be the first visitor from the Payne family.[18]

10

1811
Mary Anne Rejoins her family

It was three years since Randolph had left his school at Brighton. He was lucky to have been given a job at Court where he was known as a ward of the late Admiral Payne. Recently Frederick had joined him and they worked together from St James's Palace. Most of their work was for the Gentleman of His Majesty's Wine Cellars. The two young men had lodgings nearby but were able to spend much of their free time at Sherwood Lodge with their family.

When Randolph expressed interest in making the trip, his master encouraged him to do so because he saw this as a chance to get a good report on the wine situation in France. The war was not expected to last long; it would be most advantageous to make an early contact with the suppliers they had dealt with in the past and to start shipments with the minimum delay.

When the day came, Maria and Randolph set off in Maria's own carriage for Margate where they could stay with friends until they sailed. Traffic between England and France was, in theory, non-existent but some ships were making the journey on an irregular and unofficial basis. Maria made it known in the right quarters that she wanted to cross the Channel and would pay well. The small ship on which they were offered a passage promised a very uncomfortable crossing. The sailing ships of the day took about ten hours in favourable conditions. They were lucky and caused no consternation when, dishevelled, cold and bilious, but talking impeccable French, they stepped ashore with their baggage into Napoleon's France. Compared with Maria's own carriage, the coach which took them on the next stage of their journey to Paris was crowded, dirty, smelly and uncomfortable. Long trips by road were unpleasant and tedious. A traveller was lucky if he covered six miles in the hour and on steep inclines he was made to get out and walk, sometimes even to push. On the open road highwaymen were an ever-present fear; each coach had a guard with loaded firearms ready at his side; strangers were ordered to keep their distances and threatened at gun point if they came too near. It was an enormous relief when, at long last, they reached a large coaching inn near the centre of the capital; there they took rooms and slowly recovered from their ordeal.

When sufficiently refreshed, Maria set off to the convent in the Faubourg St Antoine to announce her arrival and to contact Mary Anne. Randolph started his investigations; to him everything was strange and fascinating; to Maria everything was changed and distressing. From the many contacts Randolph had been given before he left London, he very quickly improved his knowledge of recent French history and compiled a dossier of facts and figures which would enable him to report back to Court as required. The Revolution had not started suddenly; it had begun with relatively small incidents and gathered momentum over about three years. After the first political phase which was to break up the existing order, there followed the social phase which brought the well-known violence and atrocities with it and shocked the outside world. The three Revolutionary factions with widely differing philosophies tried to agree a new democratic constitution. In the meantime, great number of aristocrats and army officers had emigrated and with the support of Austria and Prussia they threatened to invade France and overthrow the Revolution. In the face of this threat, conscription was introduced and an army of 800,000 - a military strength of numbers which had never before been seen in Europe - was mobilized and trained. A young army Captain, Napoleon Bonaparte, made his mark at Toulon which had been captured by the British for use as a Mediterranean Naval base. With great military skill he had recaptured the town and expelled them from the port.

Earlier, the Revolutionary leaders had introduced a form of paper money and the unrestrained issue of this means of exchange had led to serious inflation and the abandonment of any attempt to meet expenditure from taxes.

Taxation was discontinued. This policy completed the country's bankruptcy, from which the only solution was to overrun France's neighbours and annex their wealth. The first of these countries was Belgium; this alarmed the British. Napoleon made rapid progress up the ladder of power, proving himself to be not only an exceptionally able army officer but also a brilliant administrator. The administration of France had become – quite literally – a shambles, when Napoleon was given a seat in the newly-formed Consulate which was trying to govern the country. In a very short time he succeeded in becoming the head of the Consulate. From this position of power he had immediately scrapped the shaky plans for a new constitution and transferred all effective power to himself as Chief Consul. The Revolution was over but the long period of war had started during which Napoleon had progressively gained domination over most of Europe.

At the time that Maria and Randolph were in Paris, his fortunes had already gone into reverse, in particular on the home front. France was returning again to a state of bankruptcy while its people were reduced to a piteous state of poverty. Those whom Randolph saw and met were sick of war, dreadfully impoverished and longing for peace. News reaching Paris from Russia – with rumours that Napoleon himself had perished – reduced the morale of the French people still further. Randolph was sure that peace would not be long coming.

Each country had tried to damage the other's economy. Britain blockaded French ports from Greece to Scandinavia, preventing the entry of goods from the New World, Africa and the East. This was very successful. France introduced the so-called 'Continental System', which discouraged the countries under Napoleon's control from trading with Britain; this was not so successful. Both policies caused some harm to the other but France suffered the most. In England there was over-production of textiles, particularly woollen cloth; prices had fallen and markets had shrunk, causing hardship, poverty and some unemployment.

In France, as well as the blockade against her exports, the value of French paper money had collapsed and products like wine and brandy could not be sold at home or abroad. The price of essentials, including food and clothing, had soared, causing great distress and near starvation. If Britain's surplus woollen cloth could be transported to France and bartered for wine and brandy this would do both customers and producers a great service and would be a profitable commercial adventure. This was the thought which made the greatest impact on Randolph's mind.

Having spent the minimum time necessary in Paris, Maria and Randolph, with Mary Anne, arrived home safely. It was necessary, in the circumstances, to allow her a few months to settle down with the Payne family and into her strange surroundings, before she was launched into society. Mary Anne appeared in Mrs Fitzherbert's company in 1812 and was introduced to her friends as her niece and adopted daughter, Marianne Smythe.

11

1808-1811
The Merchant Adventurers

All his life Randolph had associated with interesting people, and particularly in his boyhood, with such people as Admiral Jack Payne and his relatives who had played leading parts in exercising Britain's naval strength or building up her vast commercial interests in far distant parts of the world, east and west. After his exciting journey to Paris, he found his work at Court very dull. He knew that he was soon to receive his patrimony from the Secret Trust Fund. He was determined to make good use of the money, to set himself up in business and to create the means of lasting wealth for himself, the girl he wanted to marry and their descendants. He wanted excitement and intended to get that by becoming a merchant adventurer. He would go into trade, that most despised of occupations. He didn't mind being at the bottom of the snobbery order! He knew his own social position. René Payne's grandfather had founded a family fortune by being a haberdasher and Lady Horatia Seymour's grandmother had been a milliner. Woollen cloth was Britain's most valuable export and many fortunes had been founded upon it.

Randolph spent hours with his brother Frederick, relating his experiences and findings in France and this merged with the subject they so often discussed together: what to do with their lives. Frederick had considered the Army, Navy and politics but had quickly come to realize that the secrecy of his parentage would get him rejected at the first interview for any such career. For the same reason he could not become a courtier. Both of them had to face up to the fact that they were in much the same position as Roman Catholics, Quakers and

RANDOLPH PAYNE
By George Richmond R.A.
1827

other nonconformists. Their grandfather, Walter Smythe, ineligible for a commission in the British Army because of his Roman Catholic faith, had been forced, like many others, to take a commission in the Austrian Army[19]. Randolph and Frederick were quick to notice, however, that Quakers, Huguenots and others like them had turned these restrictions to their advantage; they had entered the field of industry and commerce where, because of their superior education, enterprise and intelligence, they had been extremely successful.

Randolph had first met Elizabeth New in 1808 when she was only fourteen years of age and when he lived at East End House near Parsons Green.[20] Elizabeth lived at Redbourn in Hertfordshire but frequently stayed with her uncle and his family at Chelsea[21]. The two families became very friendly and met together for parties at each other's homes. When the Paynes left East End House very suddenly in 1810 he had lost touch with her temporarily but he had invited himself to stay with the Crofts at Berkhamsted Rectory. He borrowed a horse and rode along the country lanes and bridle paths to Redbourn where he renewed his acquaintance with the News, who were surprised and delighted to see him again. From then on he and Elizabeth met often and at his twenty-first birthday party they got engaged.

A few days before his twenty-first birthday, Randolph was invited to meet the trustees of the Payne Family Trust. He was asked how he wished to receive his initial grant; in land or money? He chose to take it in money. He was called upon to take the oath of secrecy which bound him to his mother's wedding vow, which was for her to keep the secret of her marriage to the Prince of Wales, for the rest of his life. Maria and the Prince had taken each of their children into their confidence over their marriage as soon as they had become old enough to be entrusted with so grave a responsibility. The Chairman told him that £20,000 would be credited to his bank account on his twenty-first birthday, 17 September 1811.

The plan the two brothers decided upon was to buy woollen cloth in England, ship it to France, barter it for wine and brandy which they would ship back to England and sell in London. Randolph was a rich man and in a year and a half Frederick would be in the same position. There was no problem in financing their enterprise. Randolph would supply the capital to get the business going and was the senior partner. The partnership would pay him interest on the working capital he provided and they would share the profits equally. When Frederick had the funds to do so, he would buy himself an equal partnership.

They both continued to live at Sherwood Lodge but in their special circumstances it was essential to have an address of their own to operate from, particularly for any interviews or written correspondence with outsiders. Randolph bought a small terraced house in Southampton Street,[22] Covent Garden, formerly belonging to a woollen draper who became his tenant; he also took an option to purchase a commercial premises in Exeter Street nearby, with huge vaults below a three storey building.

The two brothers explored the busy London Docks full of ships plying between London, the East and West Indies, China and the Americas. They enjoyed doing so together; it introduced them to a fascinating new world where life was hard and where endeavour, risk, success and excitement were a stimulating blend of experiences. They spoke to many shipping agents, ship owners and skippers but none could offer a sufficiently dependable service with small boats to ensure the success of their project. They heard that while the cross Channel traffic by small boats to and from the Cinque Ports was continuing its revival, there was none yet from London. For Randolph's project, the Cinque Ports were too far from London, the main market, for economic bulk transport which would involve a long haul by horse-drawn waggon. Timing, however, was vital and they hoped to start within weeks.

They decided that they would have to buy their own ship, engaging a reliable captain and hired crew. They also chose a French base which would enable them to make direct shipments from the Thames to their destination in France. They accepted the advice they received and decided on Tours on the navigable River Loire.

The next stage was to travel to Tours and contact merchants they could deal with. They persuaded Maria to lend them her carriage and her coachman for a month to take them into France. After two days of preparation they set off in great style from Sherwood Lodge for the Old Kent Road and via the southern stretch of Watling Street to Margate. Their first preference was a boat which would take the whole party, including the carriage and horses. Failing that, they would have to sail alone and send the carriage back to Battersea. After several disappointments they got what they wanted, at a rather high price, but in view of the freedom of movement it would give them in France the extra price was fully acceptable. By noon the next day they had driven thirty miles into France, a country completely strange to all of them except Randolph and pretty strange to him as well. By nightfall they had reached Abbeville. They were appalled at the poverty they saw everywhere and astonished at what they could obtain in exchange for quite modest items of their personal belongings. Using the same team of horses continuously it took them seven days to reach Tours.

Their business survey was completed in seven days, at the end of which time they had signed contracts with three general merchants who were eager to exchange wine for woollen cloth. These contracts related gallons of different qualities of wines to yards of different qualities of woollen cloth. Neither Napoleon's paper money, nor Napoleon's new metric system, nor English gold sovereigns would play any part in the transactions, so a straightforward barter eliminated the vicissitudes of foreign measurement and monetary systems.

They filled all the spare spaces in their carriage with the small barrels of wines and brandy they had selected and left with their French counterparts small quantities of the various woollen cloths they had agreed to supply in exchange.

As Autumn was advancing and days were getting shorter, they travelled back at a leisurely pace, enjoying the novelty of being abroad and ensuring plenty of rest each day for the horses. They reached Sherwood Lodge at the end of October after taking two weeks on the return journey.

The wine and brandy was well received by the experts at Court and many others who tried it. They gave firm orders for large quantities at very good prices. The only problem was to meet the four months' delivery date. The transport problem had to be solved and solved quickly. Randolph was not a compulsive gambler but gambling was in his blood. He was certainly not an indecisive man. He bought a ship of suitable tonnage and engaged the skipper together with the members of the crew whom he chose to keep on with him. The next phase was relatively easy, getting delivery of huge quantities of woollen cloth to a dockside warehouse ready for the first voyage which Randolph and Frederick had decided to accompany all the way to Tours. The journey took twelve days.

It took nearly a week to complete their barter deals and load their ship with wine and brandy. They returned to London where they made their deliveries well ahead of schedule and received more repeat orders than they could accept. Randolph decided to take up his option to purchase the premises in Exeter Street* and there they started to fill the vaults with barrels of wine, and in particular with barrels of brandy, which would keep and improve in the keeping.

As a result of the first commercial trip, the two brothers decided that one of them must be based at Tours. Frederick undertook to go. He joined the next outward voyage of their ship and on arrival at Tours he stayed.

---

* *These premises remained in the possession of the Payne family business until the end of the nineteenth century.*

SOME IMPORTANT LANDMARKS IN THE SERIES OF EVENTS SO FAR

1785 Dec	*The Prince of Wales and Maria Fitzherbert secretly married.*
1786	Maria purchases Clapham House twenty miles from Brighton. A daughter born - Julia.
1790	Sir John Soane commissioned by René Payne to redesign Sulby Lodge.
1790 Sept	Randolph born.
1792	Frederick born (Spring).
1793 Nov	William born.
1794 Jun	*The Prince deserts Maria to marry Caroline.*
1794	Sulby Lodge rebuilt, becomes Sulby Hall.
1795 Jan	Mary Anne (Smythe) born.
1795	Maria buys Castle Hill, Ealing.
1796	Princess Charlotte born to Caroline.
1796	The Prince craves for Maria to return to him.
1797	*The Prince and Maria secretly reunited as Mr & Mrs Payne.*
1798	Maria sells Castle Hill, Ealing to the Duke of Kent.
1798 Nov	Minney (Seymour) born.
1800	The Prince and Maria publicly reunited.
	Maria purchases East End House, Parsons Green.
1802	Treaty of Amiens starts temporary peace.
	Mary Anne taken to Paris to be educated.
	John Croft engaged as tutor by Maria.
1803	Little George born 3 April 1803. Baptized 30 April 1804.
	Randolph goes to boarding school near Brighton.
	Temporary peace violently broken.
	Admiral Jack Payne dies.
1805	Frederick goes to boarding school.
1806	William goes to boarding school.
1808	*The Prince deserts Maria finally.*
1810	Maria sells East End House, Parsons Green.
	Maria buys Sherwood Lodge, Battersea.
	John Croft becomes Rector of Berkhamsted.
1811 Jan	The Prince becomes Regent.
1811 Jun	Maria and Randolph collect Mary Anne from Paris.
1811 Sept	Randolph reaches twenty-one years of age and receives £20,000 from the Family Trust.

12

1812-1815
Peace at last

In the eighteen years of conflict, the economic strength of Britain and the plight of the poor had been deteriorating slowly but progressively. On the advice of the Hertfords, the Regent had retained Spencer Perceval and the Tory Party in power. They were reluctant to take any measures, such as establishing a minimum wage or increases in pay, which would give a temporary relief until they caused even higher prices and consequently put even more people out of work. Their policy was that the war was the cause of Britain's economic difficulties and the best way to eliminate the distress was to concentrate every effort towards a victorious end to the conflict as speedily as possible. A safety net for the destitute had already been established. Called 'rates in aid of wages', it was administered at local level and funded out of the rates. It prevented families from dying of starvation. By the winter of 1811/12 the price of food and essentials, such as wheat, had trebled since the war began; with the loss of European markets many textile firms, particularly in the Midlands, Lancashire and Cheshire, were in difficulties. The middle classes were suffering as well as the labouring classes and the plight of the growing number of unemployed was grievous. There had been bankruptcies and angry mobs had smashed productive machinery.

Morale had reached its lowest. On the evening of 11 May 1812 John Bellington, a bankrupt commercial agent from the industrial north broke into the lobby of the House of Commons and murdered the Prime Minister, Spencer Perceval. The next morning the Regent was threatened with the same fate unless the price of bread was speedily reduced. Contrary to expectations, the Regent rose to the occasion admirably. He refused to take panic measures and settled down to the difficult task of creating a broad patriotic coalition which he believed would speedily end the trade slump caused by the denial to Britain of European markets. He had to overcome the different approaches of the two main parties: the Whigs who wanted a negotiated peace with Napoleon giving quick relief to the people's distress, and the Tories who wanted to end the war victoriously and negotiate from strength a sound and lasting peace in Europe on Britain's terms. Eventually the Regent made a surprise compromise appointment of the Earl of Liverpool as Prime Minister. Liverpool turned out to be an excellent leader. Although in home affairs he took very harsh measures against civil unrest, in foreign affairs he was very successful. He held office for fifteen years and helped the Regent to gain great prestige in Europe.

Napoleon had withdrawn many troops from Spain to reinforce his expeditionary force to Moscow. Wellington was already in the ascendancy on the Peninsular and this made his task easier. The British had been very successful in recruiting and training Portuguese, who had made excellent soldiers. The same had not applied to the Spanish who proved far more effective as irregular soldiers, conducting guerilla warfare against the long supply lines which the French had to protect, absorbing most of their 300,000 men. The British supply lines, on the other hand, were by sea and short distances across Portugal. Wellington's 30,000 men and their Portuguese and Spanish supporters were slowly driving the 300,000 French Army out of Spain. News of these successes were very good for the morale of the long-suffering British at home.

War broke out in North America when an attack was made on Canada. Because Napoleon's star was in decline, England was able to release troops and ships from Europe and concentrate them with great success on America. The blockade of the French coast was no longer so necessary and was relaxed. Randolph's enterprise benefited from this improved freedom of the seas between Britain and France.

The Regent attracted intense unpopularity over his treatment of Princess Caroline and his hatred of her became a mania. Popular feeling was wholly on her side and crowds in the street made their feelings known by cheering her and her daughter enthusiastically. In contrast, crowds in the streets, the press and Caroline herself all demonstrated and spoke against the Regent. He would have liked to have divorced Caroline and marry again, in the hope that he could have a son. That would rid him of his detested wife and depose his rebellious daughter.

But the Regent already had four legitimate Protestant sons whom he had kept secret for twenty-one years. The eldest of these sons had just received as patrimony a very large sum of money and, at that very time, was starting out on a career in commerce. What a life the Regent could give him if only he dared; but his father, the King, might recover at any time and take over the throne again. If that happened, it would be he, the ex-Regent, not his rebellious daughter, who would be deposed. He lacked the power, popularity and courage to take such a dangerous gamble.

Despite the wars in Europe and America, the political problems of his country, the rebellious mood of his subject people and of the women in his own private life, the Regent had time to devote his attention to those absorbing interests of his life, architecture and town planning. Building and improving his own residences had brought him into contact with leading architects of the day. He was assisted by the good advice of Lord Hertford and the genius of John Nash. The plans he commissioned John Nash to draw up for the grand scale improvement of the West End of London were published in 1812.

Randolph Payne and Elizabeth New were married by special licence at St Paul's Church, Covent Garden, on 4 April 1812 at 11.30 am. Maria lent them her carriage and her house at Brighton for their honeymoon. Randolph had taken over his house, 9 Southampton Street, Covent Garden, from his tenant and he and his wife took up residence there. Maria encouraged them to return to Sherwood Lodge whenever they wanted to do so.

Randolph and Frederick continued to build up stocks of wine and brandy as fast as they could ship it to London. Frederick organized the exchange of woollen cloth for wine and brandy at Tours and the loading and unloading when their ship arrived. Randolph managed the unloading, stocking and sale of wine and brandy in London and the purchase of woollen cloth, which was available in abundance at very low prices, for shipment to Frederick.

In Spring 1813 Frederick returned to London for his twenty-first birthday party. He received his patrimony and his birthday party at Sherwood Lodge featured an abundance of wines and a choice of superb cognacs.

Two days after Frederick's birthday the two brothers closed the accounts of their business. They found that, taking into consideration the value of their buildings, ship and stocks and having allowed Randolph interest on the working capital he had sunk into the enterprise, there was a rich margin of profit to share between them. Frederick bought a half share in the business by repaying his elder brother half the working capital he had so far provided. Thus started 'Randolph Payne and Partner', Woollen Drapers of 9 Southampton Street, Covent Garden.[22]

On 25 May 1813, Randolph and Elizabeth's first child was born. She was baptized at the church where they had been married, and given the names Ann Jane after her grandmother, 'Ann Jane Payne'. Maria was one of the first to meet her new grandchild, named by her eldest son after her 'other self'.

Three months previously, in February 1813, readers of *The Morning Chronicle* were astonished to find that it contained a long 'open letter' from Princess Caroline to her husband the Regent on the subject of their seventeen year old daughter's social life. Amongst other things, she complained that her only child's permitted visits to herself, her mother, had been reduced from once a week to once a fortnight, that his policy of restricting their daughter from all intercourse with the outside world was particularly unfortunate, and that Charlotte had not yet been confirmed, although other members of the Royal Family had been, when much younger.

Princess Caroline lived mainly at Blackheath and Charlotte lived virtually as a prisoner at Warwick House, adjoining the Regent's residence, Carlton House. She went to occasional family parties at Carlton House with her father, grandmother, uncles and spinster aunts but, like her mother, she led a dull and restricted life and was thoroughly bored.

This 'open letter' had been Princess Caroline's last resort in her frustrated attempts to have direct discussions with the Regent on his treatment of their daughter. The latter caused commotion behind the scenes in Government circles and in the Regent's household, but as far as Caroline was concerned her plea was totally ignored.

After Charlotte's eighteenth birthday on 7 January 1814, both she and the Regent were for once agreed on one thing: that the only suitable course for her to take was to marry as soon as possible. The Regent's choice was the Prince of Orange, heir to the Dutch throne which Napoleon was occupying at that time. It was Britain's intention to free the Netherlands, restore the House of Orange to the throne and create a Kingdom of the United Netherlands, embracing the territories of Holland and Belgium.

The Prince of Orange had been to Oxford for two years and with the Duke of Wellington's staff in the Peninsular War. To Charlotte, he was mentally boorish and physically unattractive. She tried hard to reconcile herself to this match but was finally put off when he confided to her that he would expect her to live permanently in Holland and break her links with England, including her prospects as heir to the throne.

On 30 June Parliament doubled Princess Caroline's annual grant to £50,000. She magnanimously had this reduced to £35,000 to 'ease the burden on the taxpayer', a gesture which was hailed with delight by her partisans. However they were soon disappointed when, a few weeks later she left for Germany, declaring that as the English Court would not give her the honours due to a Princess of Wales she was content to remain 'Caroline, a happy merry soul'. For the next six years she played that part to perfection.

A year earlier Maria had been planning to travel to Tours with Minney and Marianne to visit Frederick, but Napoleon had returned ignominiously from Russia and the war was raging again dangerously near to Paris. Maria had a horror of long sea passages since, years before, she had travelled from Dieppe to Newhaven and struck a stormy patch of weather. The ship was blown off course and the trip was extra long, very uncomfortable and extremely frightening. She resolved always to cross the Channel by the short route and warned her friends and relatives to do likewise.[23] When she heard that Randolph and Frederick were sailing all the way from London to Nantes her anxiety had been overwhelming.

It was not until Napoleon's series of defeats ended in the surrender of Paris on 31 March 1814, and his own abdication soon after, that Maria turned her thoughts again to her intended trip to Tours. At about the same time that Princess Caroline left England from Shoreham-by-Sea, Maria, Marianne and Minney, who were at Brighton, were ready to go. Little George spent much of his time at Berkhamsted staying and studying with the Crofts so he would be well looked after in his mother's absence. Maria announced to her Brighton acquaintances that she was going to Paris. It so happened that the Regent was due to take his mother to the Royal Pavilion at that time to celebrate her birthday.[24] The rumour spread that Maria was leaving to avoid being there when the Prince paid one of his, now rare visits to the town. She didn't attempt to contradict this convenient rumour. The three of them did go to Margate and they did go to Paris but only for one night's rest en route to Tours.

Back in the spring of 1814, twenty-one years after the Regent as Prince of Wales had accompanied the first British contingent as it left London for the wars, he invited the Allied rulers and generals to cross from France to celebrate

Napoleon's abdication and his exile to the tiny island of Elba. The 'year of revelry' had begun.

'He had some reason to congratulate himself; he had kept from office those who had wanted a compromise peace in 1811 and he had encouraged Wellington's army when Portugal seemed so far from Paris. The rulers of Austria, Russia and Prussia had shared in the final defeat of Napoleon but they had also been his allies at earlier stages of the conflict; only Britain had consistently attacked the tyrant on land and on the oceans.

The celebrations began with the honouring of Louis XVIII on his ceremonial journey from Aylesbury to Paris, through London and Dover, including three days' stay in London and a splendid dinner at Carlton House. Louis was cheered by the rejoicing crowds at every appearance and this augured well for the State visit due to take place in seven weeks' time. The Emperor of Austria declined to attend, as he was anxious to return to Vienna, but sent his Foreign Minister to represent him. The public cheered the heroes of the day and were fascinated by the Tsar. The Regent, on the other hand, who had hoped to bask in the reflected glory of victory, received little honour from his guests and virtually none from the English press and people. He was relieved when the Tsar left from Dover and Wellington arrived in England. He honoured the general with a grand ball at Carlton House, but his own intended triumph was always blighted by the fear of hostile demonstrations against him by supporters of his detested wife.

During the celebrations, Princess Charlotte met the handsome Crown Prince of Russia and also Prince Leopold of Saxe-Coburg. She broke off her engagement with Prince William of Orange.

The Regent, disappointed with the outcome of the victory celebrations and tired of considering a suitable husband for his daughter, turned his attentions to more pressing matters. There were riots following the passing of the Corn Bill which protected home-grown corn from lower priced imports. Worse still, came reports that Napoleon had fled from Elba. While the victorious Allied sovereigns and statesmen were gathered in Congress at Vienna to thrash out a future peaceful Europe to their mutual benefit and satisfaction, Napoleon had landed in southern France, rallied the veterans of his former army to his standard and was marching on Paris to depose Louis XVIII.

'The Regent and his government faced the situation calmly. Wellington was appointed Commander of the Low Countries and left for Brussels.

On 18 June 1815 his army came face to face with Napoleon's at Waterloo. With the timely arrival of Blücher's army the great battle was won but Napoleon himself had escaped death or capture. He was taking refuge at the port of Rochefort, contemplating surrender to *HMS Bellerophon* when he wrote to the Regent:

> 'Pursued by the factions which divide my country and by the hostility of the greatest European powers, I have ended my political career and I come, as Themistocles did, to seat myself at the hearth of the British people. I put myself under the protection of its laws, which I claim from Your Royal Highness as the strongest, most consistent and most generous of my foes.'

The Regent was flattered and seriously considered giving asylum to the fallen Emperor, under some form of dignified restraint, but Lord Liverpool was not prepared to take the risk. On 8 August 1815 *HMS Northumberland,* with General Bonaparte on board, sailed to St Helena in the South Atlantic.

The 'most consistent' of his foes, the Regent, returned again to the familiar trivialities of his life. To his great relief, his daughter Charlotte had made up her mind. She declared her partiality for Prince Leopold of Saxe-Coburg; at last father and daughter were in a state of harmony.

13

1815-1819
Births & Deaths

In January 1815 Randolph and Elizabeth's second child was born, a son. He was given the name Randolph; the name his grandfather had chosen thirty years previously for his secret life as Mr Payne and had then given to his eldest son.

The period between 1816 and 1824 was crowded with family events. Thirty years earlier it had been just two people, the Prince of Wales and Mrs Maria Fitzherbert who were making family history. By 1816 there were fifteen. This was the year when William would have received his patrimony. Little has been passed down the generations concerning his adult life. It is possible that he took a country estate near Sulby Hall as part of his entitlement. With the name 'William Payne' he would have blended into the local populace without causing any curiosity. Alternatively he may have joined Frederick in France and ended his days there. He may have died before he received the legacies he would have inherited from his father and mother.

In 1816 William* was still at Sulby Hall. The city was not for him; he loved the open country, farming for a job and riding and shooting for recreation, particularly the latter. When he left school, which he only just succeeded in doing voluntarily, he spent most of his time there, helping Eleanor (Mrs George Payne) in running the estate. Maria's children and their subsequent descendants were very mixed in character, reflecting the difference between herself and her spouse. There were the solid citizens like Randolph and Frederick and the wild and happy-go-lucky 'Princes of Pleasure'. William and young George were in the latter category.

If it had not been that 'Little George' made a fifth child at Sulby Hall, whereas it was well known that George Payne's (born Pearce) widow had only four children at her husband's death six years earlier, he could have been safely absorbed into Eleanor's family; no one would have known him as any other than the son of the late George Payne*.

In his true family, that of the Prince and Maria, little George was separated from his three elder brothers by a gap of nine years and, for his education, he did not follow in their footsteps. They, all three, went to the same boarding school near Brighton, which was the scene of most of their childhood. George, on the other hand, spent most of his childhood at Parsons Green with short stays at Sulby Hall, Sherwood Lodge and with the Crofts at Berkhamsted.

The Prince had always taken a special interest in George. He had allowed this son to take his own name. He harboured the inherent upper-class distaste for people in trade and industry and felt rather guilty that his two eldest sons had gravitated to the 'tradesman' class. He was determined that his youngest son George should go to Eton and Oxford and become a country gentleman, the squire of Sulby Hall. At the age of thirteen George went to Eton[25] where he was entered in the records as George Payne, the son of George. It is significant that neither of George Pearce's two sons, William Ralph and John, went to Eton.[25]

On 1 June 1816 a second daughter, Julia was born to Randolph and Elizabeth.

---

* *If the reader is getting confused with all the George Paynes in this story, small wonder that researchers a hundred years later were hopelessly misled, as was the intention.*

Randolph's will bequeathed a miniature portrait of 'my late brother William' and a silver watch inscribed 'Wm Payne November 8th 1817'.

There is a family tradition that there was an amateur highwayman amongst the uncles. It is not impossible that William was the man and came to a bad end. He predeceased Randolph, had no heirs and was the only one of the four that could fit.

The rebuilding of the Royal Pavilion by John Nash, started in March 1815, was sufficiently completed for Queen Charlotte with two of her daughters, the Duke of Kent and Princess Charlotte to spend Christmas at Brighton with the Regent. 1816 was the year when the Princess and Prince Leopold became engaged. It was a genuine love match; on the second of May they were married at Carlton House and spent their honeymoon at the Duke of York's house, Oatlands Park. Leopold, the third son of the Duke of Saxe-Coburg-Saalfeld, had been in the Russian army when the allies entered Paris. Before his military service he had travelled widely; he had experience of the world and was well-informed. He was intellectual and studious, a good singer and a keen artist.

On 7 January 1817, the Regent gave a ball at the Pavilion for Charlotte's twenty-first birthday to which Minney was invited. On the sixteenth of the same month he gave a second ball for the Grand Duke Nicholas of Russia to which she was again invited. The twenty year old Grand Duke led off the dancing with Minney and danced with her most of the evening.

Charlotte and Leopold lived happily together at Claremont House near Esher for eighteen months when tragedy struck them; their first child was stillborn and Charlotte herself did not survive the ordeal. Prince Leopold, the Regent and the whole country were overwhelmed with grief. On 6 November 1817, the Royal family found themselves once again without an Heir-apparent.

On 1 August 1814 London had been celebrating the centenary of Hanoverian Accession in an elaborate and costly manner, a bonanza for the people of the city. Two years later there was no known legitimate Royal grandchild to succeed the middle-aged generation of Hanoverian Dukes.

The Regent was married and tragically childless and likely to remain so.

The noble Duke of York had married a suitable Royal bride, Frederika of Prussia, in 1791 but the marriage was unsuccessful; they had no children. The Duke lived with his mistress, Mary Ann Clarke, while the Duchess filled their home, Oatlands Park, with her pet dogs; 100 at one time.

The Duke of Clarence lived with Mrs Jordan, the actress, and they added ten illegitimate children to the two children of her former liaison. They had separated in 1811 because he could not afford to support their enormous family. He intended to marry a woman of great wealth but no such woman that he could find would accept his offer.

The Duke of Kent was at this time living happily with Madame de St Laurent at Castle Hill, Ealing. She had been accepted as his 'unmarried wife' for a quarter of a century. He saw where his duty lay and wrote pathetically to Mrs Fitzherbert on 1 December 1817:

> 'My ever dearest Mrs Fitzherbert,
> . . . and when to that is added all that I foresee may happen, I might add *must* happen to myself in long consequences, you may imagine how deeply all these considerations must have affected me. Thank God, owing to my abstemious mode of living, and my availing myself of the opportunity of my own little Garden affords me of taking the air, I have preserved my health, but my heart is half-broke, and, when I look at my poor companion of four & twenty years, I think we may perhaps before long be imperatively forced by my duties to my family & my Country to part, it quite distresses me, and from morning till night I hardly ever have a dry eye. But I strive to think that an all-wise Providence will direct all eventually for the best, & to await the events that may be at hand with resignation & submission . . . I hope I shall have the energy to do my duty, but the sacrifice of so much domestic comfort will be dreadful. Yet even that can only be thought of, if the means are afforded me amply according to my feelings to provide for the honourable & comfortable independence for life of that individual who has been my sole comfort & companion . . . while life lasts, I shall ever remain, my dearest Mrs Fitzherbert, your most faithfully devoted and affectionate friend.
>
> Edward.

The Duke of Cumberland was married but had produced no heirs so far.

The Duke of Sussex's unauthorized marriage had been

dissolved by his father many years previously but he considered himself still to be married.

The Duke of Cambridge was a bachelor at the time.

The newspapers were full of the need for the King's sons to marry German Princesses and produce heirs to the throne. The Dukes of Clarence, Kent and Cambridge were virtually commanded to do so and try respectably for sons. They obeyed reluctantly but wasted no time. The Duke of Clarence married Adelaide of Saxe-Meiningen. She loved children but, sadly, none of her babies lived beyond early childhood. The Duke of Kent, after Madame Laurent had retreated to a convent, married Victoria of Saxe-Coburg, Leopold's sister, a widow with two children by her former marriage. The Duke of Cambridge married Augusta of Hesse-Cassel.

The Duchess of Cambridge had a son in March 1819, Prince George. The Duchess of Kent had a daughter on 24 May 1819, PRINCESS VICTORIA.

The Hanoverian dynasty was saved at the eleventh hour from extinction, but the gallant action of the Royal Dukes was not without the supreme sacrifice. The Duke of Kent died at the early age of fifty-one, eight months after his new wife had given birth to his child.

In September 1819 William, Randolph Payne's second son, was born at his mother's home in Redbourn and baptized in London together with his sister Elizabeth, born the previous year.

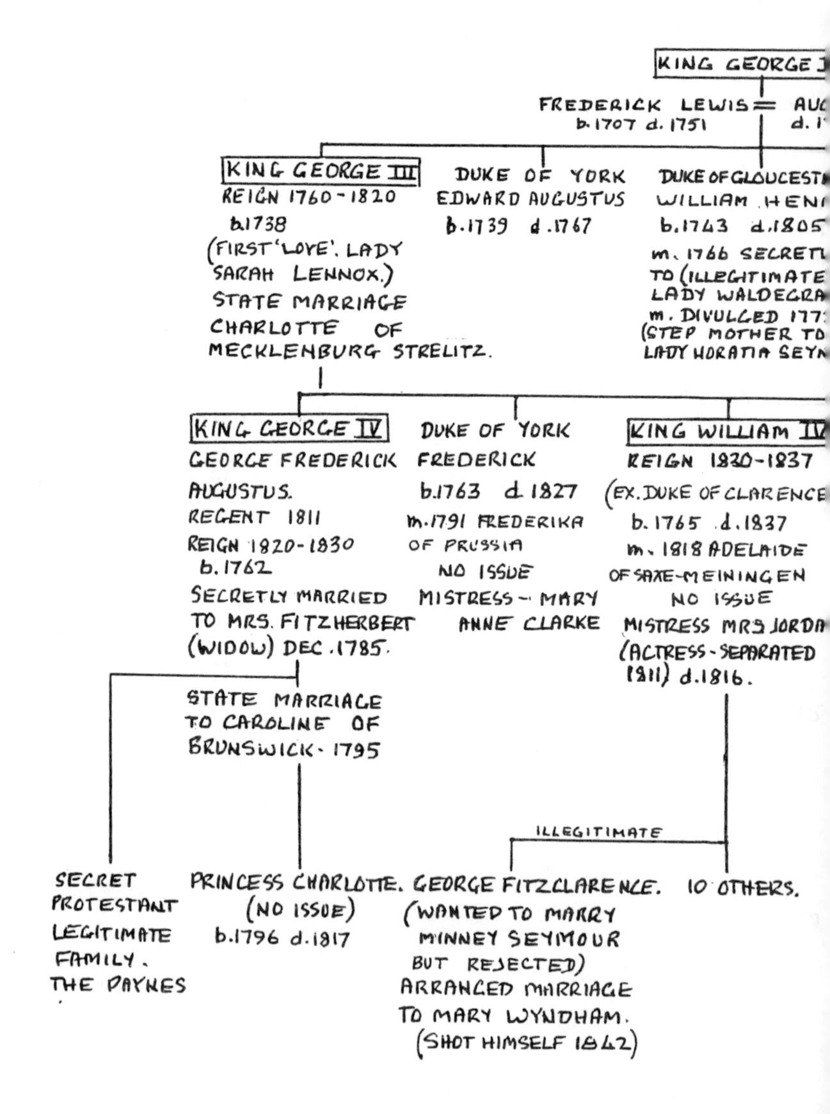
KING GEORGE I
FREDERICK LEWIS b.1707 d.1751
AU
d.1
KING GEORGE III
REIGN 1760-1820
b.1738
(FIRST 'LOVE'. LADY SARAH LENNOX.)
STATE MARRIAGE CHARLOTTE OF MECKLENBURG STRELITZ.
DUKE OF YORK
EDWARD AUGUSTUS
b.1739 d.1767
DUKE OF GLOUCEST
WILLIAM HEN
b.1743 d.1805
m. 1766 SECRETL
TO (ILLEGITIMATE
LADY WALDEGRA
m. DIVULGED 177
(STEP MOTHER TO
LADY HORATIA SEY
KING GEORGE IV
GEORGE FREDERICK AUGUSTUS.
REGENT 1811
REIGN 1820-1830
b.1762
SECRETLY MARRIED TO MRS. FITZHERBERT (WIDOW) DEC.1785.
STATE MARRIAGE TO CAROLINE OF BRUNSWICK. 1795
DUKE OF YORK
FREDERICK
b.1763 d.1827
m.1791 FREDERIKA OF PRUSSIA
NO ISSUE
MISTRESS - MARY ANNE CLARKE
KING WILLIAM IV
REIGN 1830-1837
(EX. DUKE OF CLARENCE
b.1765 d.1837
m. 1818 ADELAIDE OF SAXE-MEININGEN
NO ISSUE
MISTRESS MRS JORDA
(ACTRESS - SEPARATED 1811) d.1816.
ILLEGITIMATE
SECRET PROTESTANT LEGITIMATE FAMILY. THE PAYNES
PRINCESS CHARLOTTE. (NO ISSUE) b.1796 d.1817
GEORGE FITZCLARENCE. (WANTED TO MARRY MINNEY SEYMOUR BUT REJECTED) ARRANGED MARRIAGE TO MARY WYNDHAM. (SHOT HIMSELF 1842)
10 OTHERS.
THE CAUSE AND EF

E–GOTHA

E OF CUMBERLAND
NRY FREDERICK
745 d. 1790
IRS HORTON 1771
OW. NO ISSUE

OTHERS

DUKE OF GLOUCESTER
FREDERICK WILLIAM

PRINCESS SOPHIA
NO ISSUE

DUKE OF KENT
EDWARD
b1767 d1820
MISTRESS
MADAME DE ST. LAURENT
(FRENCH CANADIAN)
FOR 27 YEARS.
m. 1818 VICTORIA
OF SAXE-COBURG

DUKE OF CUMBERLAND.
ERNEST.
b.1771 d.1851
KING OF HANOVER
1837.

DUKE OF CAMBRIDGE
ADOLPHUS
b.1774 d.1850
m.1818 (WHEN 42)
AUGUSTA OF
HESSE-CASSEL

DUKE OF SUSSEX
AUGUSTUS FREDERICK.
b.1773 d.1843
SECRETLY MARRIED LADY
AUGUSTA MURRAY
(DAUGHTER OF EARL
OF DUNMORE) IN
ROME APRIL 1793
REMARRIED IN LONDON.
MARRIAGE DISSOLVED
BY GEORGE III FOR
BREACH OF ROYAL
MARRIAGE ACT.
CHILDREN DECLARED
ILLEGITIMATE

OTHERS

QUEEN VICTORIA
REIGN 1837–1901
b. 1819

DUKE OF CAMBRIDGE.
b. 1819

TWO
DAUGHTERS

SIR AUGUSTUS D'ESTE.

LADY TRURO

OF THE ROYAL MARRIAGE ACT OF 1772
HANOVERIAN DYNASTY

14

1819-1824
King George IV and his family

In November 1819 Minney was twenty-one; since 'coming out' and having become a polished young lady, she had a train of enamoured gentlemen in tow, one of whom was George Fitzclarence, the eldest son of Mrs Jordan and the Duke of Clarence. He had fallen in love with her when she was only twelve years old and had loved her ever since. Minney had not the heart to reject his hand decisively and he continued to pursue her. Though his father was in favour of the match the Regent and Mrs Fitzherbert were not; perhaps, amongst other considerations, because they knew that they were first cousins. Minney wanted a dashing hero and relegated him to the shelf of dear dullards. Eventually the Duke of Clarence arranged for him to marry Mary Wyndham, one of the six natural children of the third Earl of Egremont.

Minney Seymour was very much in the public eye as would be expected of a girl of her age, beauty and position. Sir George Seymour, Lady Horatia's eldest son, felt responsibility for her and when gossip reached his ears he expressed his concern to Maria. In addition to the 'enamoured gentlemen she had in tow', she was often to be seen in public with one or more of Maria's sons – her true brothers – walking, talking and laughing merrily together in a boisterous and uninhibited manner. To the gossips she was a young unchaperoned, single lady enjoying the company of unknown young men – probably men of low birth – 'strangers'.

This was difficult for poor Maria to explain and she wrote to Sir George:

> '. . . there is not the smallest reason for the reports that have been so industriously circulated concerning her. She is certainly an object of attraction and particularly so in the confined circle and if a Man happens to speak to her or is seen to join her walking it immediately sets people talking. We are rather too fond of attracting admiration but in this instance I have really no particular fault to find. It is natural at her age to like being admired and I hope with her good sense as she grows older, that that love of flirtation will rebate . . . Let me beg of you to contradict this absurd report which vexes me very much and certainly it is detrimental to her and really I don't know how it is to be avoided unless I lock her up in her room and never let her see a human being.'

'Strangers' became a code word in the family circle and Maria used it in her letter from Brighton to Minney dated 14 December 1823:

> '. . . You will be welcomed here by more than myself, for I have given out that I shall not receive company until your ladyship makes your appearance. There are several strangers here, who don't know what to do with themselves and they will be very glad to have a lounging place for dinner and for one evening. But I am determined not to kill the fatted calf until you arrive, and if as I hope, you will arrive on Saturday, I will have some company to meet you at dinner on Sunday. Therefore pray send me a line to say you will be with me that day.'

Surely, if Maria had people at her house whom she wanted Minney to make a special effort to travel down to Brighton to meet, she would have said who they were. Unnamed 'strangers' are no great attraction and hardly provide 'company' who could join Maria in welcoming Minney to Maria's own house! On the other hand, if for 'strangers' one reads 'Paynes' it all makes sense.

At Eton from 1816 to 1822 'Little George' became a rebellious and boisterous opponent of school discipline. In 1822 he left Eton and moved to Christchurch College, Oxford.* There, his high spirits took charge; he led his fellow students into a riotous life with emphasis on drinking and gambling.He said that his only College at Oxford was The Mitre Hotel! He gained the reputation of being one of the pluckiest riders across country from Chipping Norton to Bicester. He indulged his sporting tastes so freely that the College authorities, after much delay and long suffering, and nine days after his twentieth birthday celebrations which were the last straw, requested him to leave; in other words, on 12 April 1823 he was 'sent down'.

George Payne returned to his family home, Sherwood Lodge, where he was subjected to the sobering influence of his mother, his eldest brother, thirteen years his senior, and his two elder sisters, Marianne and Minney. His father arranged for him to have a junior position in Court where he spent much of his time, but where his duties were extremely light, enabling him to indulge in his favourite pastimes of gambling, racing and drinking. He got on very well with courtiers and ladies-in-waiting of all ages, who found this amusing and attractive young man to be a very refreshing influence in their otherwise stuffy environment.[26] Having reached the age of twenty-one, George was elected to Brook's Club on 4 May 1824. He was proposed and seconded by Lord Kensington and Lord Sefton;[27] the latter was the son of Maria's life long friend and close relative, Lady Sefton.

During the year before his coming of age, young George was invited to a meeting by the executors of the late René Payne.[13] They told him that he had inherited a large legacy when his 'father' had died in 1810 and this had been held in trust for him until he reached the age of twenty-one. George's natural honesty prompted him to declare that he was not George Pearce's son and the money should go to Eleanor Payne and her four children. He remembered just in time that

---

* *John Croft's college.*

such a statement would be a breach of faith with his real parents so he merely thanked them for the information and immediately reported the matter to Maria. Maria was astonished at this extraordinary side effect of her great secret. She decided to consult Lord Carrington and arranged an early meeting with him. She and George attended his office in the City and George told him the facts.

Lord Carrington had been the late George (Pearce) Payne's guardian until he came of age, after which he had nothing to do with his affairs. They all agreed that his widow, Eleanor Payne and her four children, not young George, were the rightful heirs to this fortune. It was agreed that George should accept the fortune and hand it to the Payne Family Trust. Eleanor would then decide how it should be distributed.

George came of age on 3 April 1824 and received his patrimony from the Trust. He elected to have property instead of money and asked for Sulby Hall estate, which, he said, would remain the family home for Maria, Eleanor and their children for as long as they wished. George then returned to Sulby Hall where he intended to celebrate his twenty-first birthday. He had not been back to the estate for several years.

On 17 November 1818 the Regent's mother, Queen Charlotte, died. He was so deeply depressed that his own health collapsed and he was confined to Carlton House for a month. Although in his youth she had treated him severely, she had always been friendly to Maria and she had in common the Regent's dislike of Caroline. Their relationship, since her son became Regent, had been warmly affectionate and good-humoured.

From what historians have been able to glean from surviving letters, the next few years were dominated for Maria by Minney's love affairs, which gave her the utmost trouble and misery. Minney was an exquisite and amusing young lady; lovers, swains and admirers she had in plenty. The ambition of both Maria and the Regent was for a grand marriage; a Prince charming, a Duke desirable or possibly a mere Peer. In 1819 Minney fell for George Dawson (later

Damer) a good-looking and romantic young army officer who had been wounded when serving with distinction at the battle of Waterloo, but was only the younger son of an Irish Peer. Not only had he no title or property, but it was rumoured that he was in debt and a gambler. Every obstacle was put in their way.

Few people spared a thought for King George III yet everyone accepted his existence as part of the natural order. He was in the sixtieth year of his reign and hardly any of his subjects could remember a different sovereign. He was deaf, blind, mad and over eighty years of age when he died on 29 January 1820. The Regent was in a poor state of health when, in the forecourt of Carlton House, he was declared solely and rightfully the ruler of his British domains. The new King, George IV, was advised by his doctors not to attend his father's funeral. He travelled down to Brighton for two months' convalescence. This, however, was not peaceful; now he was King, Caroline, 'the happy, merry soul' had become his Queen-Consort and likely to return to England from her sordid and exhibitionist perambulations around the flesh-pots of Europe, to claim her rights. At the same time there was civil unrest in the country and a group of conspirators, who planned to murder the entire Cabinet and provoke a general insurrection, was arrested in London. Caroline DID return and was cheered by the excited crowds as she made her progress from Dover to London but when on the seventh of June she reached Carlton House, the King was not at home to meet her. By her return at this troubled time, she rendered her one service to the nation. Cheering the Queen's cause was a simpler emotional response for the mob of malcontents than continuing a campaign of menace or violence. The Queen's affairs absorbed the attention of the nation and civil unrest subsided.

The Coronation took place on 19 July 1821. The King applied all his gifts of showmanship to its planning.* It was a

* *The Earl Marshal, who assists the monarch in arranging Royal ceremonial outside the Palace, lived at Arundel Castle and had for long*

The Royal Pavilion, Brighton. The East Front.
From an aquatint in John Nash's
Views of The Royal Pavilion Brighton, 1826

remarkable triumph for his sense of majesty and a colourful and noisy day for his subjects to remember. Within twelve days he started State visits to Ireland, Scotland and Hanover. So impressive was this succession of pageantry that even the Queen was forgotten. She could no longer arouse hostility against her husband.

On 7 August 1821 Queen Caroline died and was buried in Germany in accordance with her wishes. From then on the King's major problems were those of the nation and, apart from his health, not his personal troubles. On account of an agonizing attack of gout he spent most of the next winter and much of the spring of 1822 in Brighton. The latest rebuilding of the Royal Pavilion, to John Nash's design, including the installation of gas lighting from the magnificent gasoliers and lamps in the music and banqueting rooms had, at last, been completed. Relieved from paying £35,000 per year to his

---

been part of the Prince of Wales' and Maria's social circle at Brighton.

detested wife, he increased Maria's annuity to £10,000.

Randolph's business had been thriving during the 'Year of Revelry' in 1814 and again for the Coronation and State visits of 1821.

In 1822 his children ranged from two to nine years of age, spending much of their time at Sherwood Lodge. The two eldest spent long terms at Berkhamsted being tutored by the Crofts as George had been; there was only ten years between him and his niece Ann Jane. Since William had been born, Elizabeth had no more children so, when in April 1823 she announced that she was with child again, everyone was delighted.

On 17 October 1823 their third son was born. It had been a very long and difficult delivery; both the child and Elizabeth were much weakened and her nurse and doctor became anxious. She was just strong enough to confirm the names they had chosen for their new son, Frederick Croft: Frederick after Randolph's brother and Croft as a compliment to their old and much respected family friend, the Reverend John Croft. When he was seven weeks old she died. Maria hastened to her son's assistance and took the elder children back to Sherwood Lodge, leaving Randolph with the new born baby under the care of the nurse and doctor. The baby was baptized at St Paul's, Covent Garden. Soon after Christmas the child died and was buried in his mother's grave.*

Randolph himself remained at his little home near Covent Garden and endeavoured to drown his sorrows in his work. There was a lot for him to do. So far it had been adequate to sell his wines to customers with large cellars, including the Court, and in bulk to retailers. However, as competition built

---

* *It was this tragedy of their mother's death in 1823 that brought Randolph's five children under the maternal care of Maria, their grandmother. The elder children already knew her well as their grandmother but for the two youngest, Maria was the only mother-figure of their early childhood memories.*

A story passed down through the generations came from William's daughter Katharine. She told her children that her father spoke of the occasions he well remembered from his early childhood when he would be held up to his nursery window when the King came to call and the nurse saying, 'Look! Here comes your grandpapa!'.

up, he and Frederick had decided to establish retail outlets which were within walking distance of smart residential areas. The first of these was 3 Little Tower Street under the name 'Frederick Payne' and a second at 7 Little Bruton Street under the name 'Randolph Payne'.

The need to barter wine for cloth had long since ended as French currency stabilized. Randolph Payne & Partner became a prosperous export/import business continuing to deal mainly in woollen cloth and wine. The expedient of operating their own ship, in the early days of their adventure, was no longer necessary. Means of transport by sea and land had returned to normal.

With his children in the care of Maria and her domestic staff at Sherwood Lodge, Randolph had time to travel both on business and for pleasure. Contrary to supposition, the King and Maria continued to have a friendly relationship in private and he took a great interest in his grandchildren.

Frequent visits to the Continent by Maria, Marianne and Minney at this period, alone or together, are well-documented in surviving letters. Although there is no record of Randolph going with them, it is very likely that he did sometimes do so and that Tours would have been one of the places they visited. A letter dated September 1824 mentions that Minney met Frederick[28] and one dated 17 October 1825 mentions her as passing through Nantes.[28]

15

1824-1825
Romances

Little George's twenty-first birthday party took place at Sulby Hall on 3 April 1824. It was a fabulous entertainment to which his friends from Eton, Oxford and London and the nobility of the county for miles around came in great numbers. George's ownership of the Sulby estate was announced when his toast was proposed, confirming what local people had expected for many years. His ownership of the estate brought him a handsome rental income. Everything for the young man was rosy except for one unbearable obstacle to his happiness; the little friend of his childhood, who until three weeks previously he had not seen since she was eleven years of age, matured into a most attractive girl, two years his junior, living under his own roof and with whom he had fallen hopelessly in love, was Elizabeth Martha Payne. She counted, in the false situation in which he had been placed, as his SISTER!

The chequered progress of the romance between Minney and George Dawson continued amidst floods of tears and endless beseechings. While his family were excited at the possible match, Maria and the King were resolutely opposed to it. Their precious Minney had been raised to make a spectacular marriage. She herself was torn between the misery she suffered from distressing her beloved 'Mama' and her determination not to give up the man she loved.

Maria took Minney to Paris to separate the two lovers but George followed them. A battle of wits continued until, in November 1822 Lt Colonel Dawson was posted to the West Indies; not, however, before he had remembered his rich, childless and adoring aunt, Lady Caroline Damer, who had previously helped him out of financial difficulties. She had two immense properties in Dorset and a large London house. She thought that the blood of three Irish lords should suffice even if Miss Seymour was the King's daughter. In April 1824 she came to their rescue. She told George Dawson that, owing to Mrs Louise Damer's recent death, by the terms of her own will, he would inherit Came House and all the property belonging to it, provided that the marriage (to Minney) was approved and the promised fortune was paid (by the King). She made it George Dawson's task to see that the King and Mrs Fitzherbert heard of this.

The trump card played by Lady Caroline Damer had its intended effect. The King reluctantly agreed to the marriage. In the 'season' of 1824 they were allowed to consider themselves engaged. The promised fortune from the King, amounting to £20,000, was placed in the hands of trustees and 'settled entirely, solely and only upon her (Minney) and upon any children she may probably have hereafter'. A week before the marriage, George Dawson described the terms as 'unusual, degrading and clearly betraying a want of confidence in me'.

The wedding took place on 20 August 1825. Mrs Fitzherbert did not attend the ceremony, but she bought the happy couple a house in Upper Grosvenor Street near to her own house in Tilney Street.

To all the eager onlookers this was the climax of a four year drama. This poor old lady who had suffered frustrated motherhood all her life was, after a heartrending struggle to prevent it, about to lose her adored adopted child, the one ray of sunshine in an otherwise fruitless womanhood. They were about to see Mrs Fitzherbert disappear tragically from the glamorous scene of opulent society into miserable retirement.

But when the curtain went up on the next act, an instant transformation had taken place, an unbelievable resilience was displayed. She set off on a cheerful tour of visits with her friends in the stately homes of England. Later observations, based on letters, showed that the mutual affection between herself and Minney after the trials and tribulations of recent years had not suffered at all. She sent her a light-hearted letter on her honeymoon enclosing a generous gift for her 'to spend in Paris on hats and bonnets', saying that she 'wished it could have been thousands not hundreds.' As for the object of all her agitation, she became completely reconciled to him as a son-in-law who could henceforth do no wrong.[29]

What had happened? Had she switched her attention to her recently acquired protégée Marianne Smythe whose quiet arrival on the scene had seemed such a mystery? No! She merely continued her total absorption in her large and ever-increasing secret family. There was lots for her to do; to find a husband for Marianne (a Roman Catholic), to find a wife for her widower son, Randolph, with five young children to bring up alone and to find a wife for young George.

Maria said goodbye to her five motherless grandchildren at Sherwood Lodge, having offered Randolph the use of her house in Brighton in her absence. She bought new clothes for Marianne and herself and in a cheerful mood the two mounted their carriage at Tilney Street. The horses moved off towards Watling Street at a brisk trot, destined for the first stately home on their programme of visits: that of her youngest son, George Payne of Sulby Hall.

With the easier trading and transportation conditions, Frederick's job became less complicated. He enjoyed the visits of his mother, sisters and brother to Tours but he also travelled back to England quite frequently staying at 9 Southampton Street or at Sherwood Lodge. He and Randolph decided to split their partnership so that he could exploit a wider market while Randolph could obtain wines from other sources also. This amicable new arrangement did not affect their very close cooperation.

In 1825 Frederick became engaged to Mademoiselle Maria Leur. He brought her to England to meet his family and they decided to get married before they returned to France. The wedding took place on 19 June 1825 at St Paul's Church, Covent Garden, by special licence; the marriage records list Randolph as being one of the witnesses. This deliberately modest ceremony was followed by a most memorable party at Sherwood Lodge and once again Maria lent the happy couple her carriage and her Brighton house for the honeymoon.

Frederick's first son was born three and a half years later and was given the name 'Randolph'. His second son was born on 21 February 1831 and named 'Frederick Croft', following Randolph's example of honouring the Reverend John Croft. For both baptisms he gave their business address, 9 Southampton Street, and the occupation of woollen draper. Frederick and his wife had five children altogether.[22]

16

1825-1878
George Payne of Sulby Hall

When Maria arrived at Sulby Hall Eleanor told her how she had distributed the fortune which René Payne's executors had wrongly awarded to George. She expressed the hope that her eldest son, William Ralph, would buy himself an estate in the shires when he came of age.*

She then broke the news of George's relationship with her daughter Elizabeth Martha. She explained that they were in love and that George had sworn that he would never marry any other girl and her daughter would not look at any other man. Her other worry was that, one day, someone would notice that she had five children; not the four she was known to have had at her husband's tragic death. Maria offered to ask Frederick if he would have John at Tours as his assistant and after a short exchange of correspondence this was arranged. Within a few months John had joined Frederick and was learning the job. Eleanor's family at Sulby was reduced to four again!

The situation with George was most worrying to Maria. People were already wondering how it was that a young man of his exceptional charm, popularity and worldly endowment remained unmarried despite the numerous eligible young ladies who laid themselves at his feet. If George declared publicly that there was no impediment to their marriage, it

---

* *Her eldest son bought Pitstone Hall where he lived until he died in 1859.*[8] *He had been called William Ralph to distinguish him from Maria's son, the other William of Sulby Hall, but historically they got confused.*

would put the family secret at risk. They wanted to continue to live in the district and in the home they loved. It was eventually decided that their only recourse was to pay someone to give Elizabeth a respectable married name and for them to live together as man and wife. George's situation was somewhat unique, but similar and less innocent expedients were not unknown, particularly in the private lives of Royal Dukes and Princes.

George engaged an agent to find a man who needed money urgently, wanted status, not a wife, and was prepared to sell the use of his name.

In 1827 at the age of twenty-two Elizabeth Martha Payne assumed the name 'Mrs Holyoake'. There is no mention in the Welford Parish Records of this marriage. Soon after, her 'brother' George Payne made substantial extensions to his home, Sulby Hall. On 28 January 1830 the Parish Records of Welford registered the baptism of Francis Lyttleton son of Francis Lyttleton Holyoake and Elizabeth Martha of Sulby. This child may have died in infancy. In 1833 Francis Holyoake succeeded to his father's estate at Studley in Warwickshire, and built a house which he called Studley Castle. He assumed the name 'Goodricke'. Two years later he was created first Baronet of Studley Castle. Elizabeth Martha became Lady Goodricke. In 1836 Elizabeth had a son, Harry, who was educated at Rugby School and entered the 90th Light Infantry at the age of eighteen. He served in the Crimean War and was severely wounded, receiving the Crimean medal and clasp. Elizabeth had a third son, George, and four daughters.

In 1842 Sir Francis Goodricke became Master of the Pytchley Hunt, which fulfilled another of his ambitions. By 1863 he was bankrupt and had to sell Studley Castle. Two years later he died and Harry Goodricke became the second Baronet.

George Payne of Sulby became a very well-known figure in the hunting, racing and gambling world and much has been written about him, mostly in retrospect. In *The Dictionary of National Biography* the earliest source of information was the 'Sporting Magazine' of 1837 when he was thirty-four and *'The Illustrated News'* of 1844. Other information comes from much later bibliography and would have come largely from legend.

He was always portrayed as a mystery and the subject of much colourful gossip and rumour, 'A man who was spoken of with affection, respect and almost with reverence . . .[30] He was a man who might have done anything and did nothing; still he was loved and looked up to by all who knew him, as the sealed pattern of the perfect gentleman.' Another biographer writes: 'There never has been and never will be but one George Payne – a stalwart form, handsome countenance, winning smile, and a charm of manner never equalled, took captive all who came within the circle of their attraction. It would scarcely be going too far to say that no man ever possessed in the same degree a similar gift of making himself acceptable to all sorts of persons. It seemed as though he could at all times reach the soft spot in anyone's heart, be they of either sex, or in any condition of life.[30] Heir to a fine place and a splendid fortune, and endowed with abilities of no common order, it is no wonder that he entered public life as a sort of "Prince Camaralzaman" . . .'[30]

On George's spending and gambling excesses much has also been written: 'He came of age in 1824 and into possession of the family seat, Sulby Hall, with a rent roll of £17,000 a year . . . the money disappeared in a few years together with two other large inheritances from relatives.'*

'He seems to have set out to spend as fast as possible. His coming-of-age party was fabulous.[26]

'About this Northamptonshire character a special book could be written. His colourful life encompassed a drama** as exciting as many a stage plot. As a betting man he must have been the biggest mug in history. Sometimes he would back nearly every horse in a race and still manage to miss the winner. In 1824 he lost £33,000 on one horse'.[26]

'In 1824 he lost £20,000 on the St Ledger'. (A different figure from the other biographer.)[31]

---

* *It is Payne family tradition that one of the uncles owned racehorses; lost three fortunes racing and gambling; drank enough to float a battleship and spent enough to buy one.*

George, being the youngest, would have received his patrimony and the legacies from his mother and father within the short period of thirteen years. He was probably thought locally to own all the land belonging to the Secret Trust, not Sulby estate alone.

GEORGE PAYNE OF SULBY,
Master of the
Pytchley Hunt
1844-1848

'His ruling passion was racing and gambling'.[30]

'Payne's gambling had by this time eaten up most of his patrimony . . .'[30]

'He was an infatuated gambler not only on the turf but also at the card table'.[31]

George Payne was Master of the Pytchley Hunt from 1835 to 1838 and then again, succeeding Sir Francis Goodricke, from 1844 to 1848.

He is described in *The Huntsman*, Volume XLIV as: . . . 'the very handsomest man I ever saw. From top to toe, he was and is the perfect model of an English gentleman. His face was clear and open, his eyes were grey, with dark lashes,

---

** *This could refer either to his parentage or to his love life, or both!*

expressive then only of excitement – at other times of purest good nature. He was about five feet eleven, and weighed about twelve stone. His dress was perfection; utterly free from the smallest taint of dandyism, it was admirably adapted for the business in hand and the person it adorned. There was no modern invention of beard and moustache, which reduces even a decent looking fellow to somewhat of the calibre of a rat-catcher's dog. His well curled black whiskers matched his short curled hair.'

William Ralph was the exact opposite of his handsome 'brother' George. He was short and round with short thighs and a very bad seat. He was, however, always amusing and indomitably cheerful. George and Ralph were great companions.[30]

George's true brother William was between nine and ten years his senior but there were strong ties of kinship between them. For both, Sulby Hall was his spiritual home and their periodical separations from one another when at different schools at different times and from the rest of their family, drew them together. George and Billy were a devoted couple.

The cause and date of William's death is not known but George's loss of his brother, his father in 1830 and his mother in 1837 would have come within a short period of time. It is very likely that it was these events that led him to resign his mastership of the Pytchley Hunt and to move his true family to a far off neighbourhood where they could shake off the burden of secrecy and escape the bestirring whispers of gossip. Railways had introduced quick and comfortable travel over long distances. George still owned valuable farming properties in Northamptonshire and attended to the progressive disposal of land owned by the Family Trust for distribution to his brothers and sisters. It was at the end of his second term of Mastership, when, in 1847, he sold Sulby Hall. His successor as Master was Viscount Alford of Ashridge near Berkhamsted (heir to Earl Brownlow).

At the age of seventy-five George Payne died at 10 Queen Street, Mayfair. In his will, made a month before his death, he left nearly all that he possessed, valued for probate at £35,000, to his sister, Lady Elizabeth Martha Goodricke. His will did not record her address. The mystery of his family life remains undisclosed.

George was buried in Kensal Green cemetery among the rich and famous of his time. The Prince of Wales, later King Edward VII, attended his funeral, which was reported in every newspaper in the country. Later, a magnificent memorial cross was erected over his grave.* The inscription on the front of the monument reads:

GEORGE PAYNE
Born at Sulby 3rd April, 1803.
Died at Queen Street, Mayfair on 2nd September 1878.

Probably unnoticed and five years later, another name was engraved on the back of the memorial:

and his nephew
Sir HARRY GOODRICKE Bart.
Born at Studley Castle, Warwickshire, August 7th 1836.
Died London October 25th 1883.

With Sir Harry's death the title died out.

---

* *The Memorial to the two men can still be seen in the overgrown and derelict cemetery at Kensal Green in north-west London.*

17

1825-1829
Randolph's Successful Holiday

Soon after Maria's departure for Sulby Hall, Randolph left his little family in the care of the very competent staff at Sherwood Lodge, and set off in his own carriage for a short stay in Brighton. One of his engagements was to play cricket with the Old Boys of his former school. He had been in the school team himself and he was a very useful batsman and fielder. He was a handsome man in his mid-thirties, still of youthful appearance and, despite the tragedy he had recently suffered, he had the light-hearted good humour which was the characteristic of all of Maria's children. The game was an annual reunion in which he had often taken part. He met many old friends with their wives and families. Sir Percy Wyndham was watching the game and recognized Randolph immediately. He was the Earl of Egremont's brother and as far back as 1784 he had rented the Prince of Wales his first house in Brighton, Grove House.[32] He had remained a close friend of the Prince of Wales, Mrs Fitzherbert and the late Admiral Jack Payne. He was fully aware of Randolph's true identity.

The 'friendly' match which Sir Percy arranged annually against the Town, was due to be played on The Steyne in three days time and one of his players had dropped out. Randolph was delighted when Sir Percy invited him to fill this gap in the team and accepted most gratefully.

On the day of the match, Randolph snatched victory out of defeat for Sir Percy's team by a strong eighth wicket stand with his fellow batsman called Willis. He scored sixty-five runs including two sixes, one of which broke a window in the

Vicar's carriage. (The Vicar received a dozen bottles of Napoleon brandy as a mark of Randolph's concern.)

Randolph and Mr Willis were still batting when the teams left the field for tea and the two men walked back to the pavilion together. The older man invited Randolph to his family's table where they joined Mrs Willis and her daughter Mary Anne for tea. Mrs Willis was a connection of the Wyndham family. She had married the Agent of Sir Thomas Wyndham's Glamorgan estate, Dunraven Castle, and Mary Anne, their daughter, had been baptized at St Brides, Glamorgan.[33] At this time Mary Anne was twenty-two years of age; they were living near Petworth but were staying in Brighton for the summer season. Randolph was swept into the social whirl of Brighton society, during which he and Mary Anne found themselves together on several occasions. Their holiday friendship warmed into a holiday romance and did not end when Randolph left Brighton to return to his little family. Later, at Battersea, Mary Anne met Randolph's five motherless children. She was very sweet to them and they returned her affection in a noisy and uninhibited manner.

While Mrs Fitzherbert continued her travels around England, constantly on the alert for suitable spouses for her unmarried children, her eldest son had done it himself. On her return to Sherwood Lodge, Randolph introduced his mother to his fiancée.

Mary Anne and Randolph were married at Kennington Church (not far from Sherwood Lodge) on 12 August 1826, a year after they had met. They spent their honeymoon with all Randolph's children at Clapham House, where he had spent so much of his early childhood. Maria had kept it for sentimental reasons, letting it to friends from time to time and lending it to her family. Randolph had earned himself a permanent place in Sir Percy Wyndham's cricket team for the annual friendly match against the Town; he never did quite so well again, although the Vicar's carriage was always to be seen close to the boundary line.

The following year, in 1827, the Court Guide reported that R. Payne Esq. was living at 11 Salisbury Place, Marylebone, a house with a garden reaching to 'New Road' (now Marylebone Road) which was then the northern fringe of a Regency development of residential properties. New Road and

Salisbury Place were on the edge of London; beyond, to the north, was the new Regent's Park and then open country with fields, trees, hedgerows, grazing cattle and farm buildings.

On 16 June 1828 Marianne Smythe married the Hon. Edward Stafford Jerningham, a Roman Catholic.* Maria's perambulations had not been entirely in vain!

On 10 July 1829 Mary Anne Payne gave birth to her first child whom she and Randolph named Frederick Wyndham.** Their next child was called Mary Anne, primarily in honour of her mother but, conveniently also, in honour of her grandmother (née Mary Anne Smythe) and her aunt (née Mary Anne Smythe).

Randolph and his second wife had eleven children.

---

* *Their children were:*
1) Augustus Frederick Stafford Jerningham, tenth Lord Stafford.
2) Fitzherbert Edward, eleventh Lord Stafford.
3) Emily, who married Basil Thomas Fitzherbert of Swynnerton. Their son was Francis Edward Fitzherbert who became the twelfth Lord Stafford. Thus Marianne produced an heir for the Fitzherberts which Maria, her mother, failed to do when the baby she bore to Thomas Fitzherbert died in infancy.
** *Frederick Wyndham Payne called* his *eldest son 'Percy Wyndham' and his third son 'Wilfred James Croft'. Many subsequent descendants, down to the present day, used the name Wyndham in honour of Mary Anne's noble connection.*

18

1830
The King's Secret Bequests

Amongst the King's many activities, it was the problems he encountered with his Royal wife and his daughter that came to the eyes of his subjects; matters which, for ordinary beings, would be part of their private and not their public life and which would normally go unnoticed. For this reason, the side of his character which made him unpopular tended to obscure his main achievements, which were going ahead unapplauded. He had been Regent for nine years and was just starting his reign as King. The public did not see him in his relaxed moments, as a man who was extremely good company, a wit, an amusing mimic, a good-natured gossip and an interesting conversationalist, well-informed on a wide range of topics. They did not see him in his Pavilion, with his stays loosened over the curaçao, laughingly entertaining his friends and relatives with impersonations of cabinet ministers or taking over as conductor of the band while singing with enthusiasm in a loud bass voice. He was a connoisseur of the arts; he was making enormous contributions to the national heritage in collections of pictures, particularly the Dutch school, exquisite furniture and *objets d'art*, particularly French. He gave his father's library of books to the nation.

George IV was the inspiration and driving force behind the ambitious improvements taking shape in London; the greatest reconstruction since the reign of Charles II after the Great Fire. He encouraged the demolition of a clutter of little streets and miserable buildings to drive a broad thoroughfare, as straight as possible, between Carlton House and the newly created Regent's Park. He was demolishing his own residence,

Carlton House, to build houses for rent, thereby financing the conversion of Buckingham House into Buckingham Palace. He had the Palladian portico of Carlton House re-erected as the frontal feature of the new National Gallery. He built Royal Lodge at Windsor, which became his final residence while converting Windsor Castle from a medieval fort into a Royal Palace up to the standards of his day. This work included the Waterloo Chamber, which was to be a tribute to the victory and a home for the portraits of allied sovereigns, statesmen, soldiers and sailors (including Admiral Jack Payne) involved in the defeat of Napoleon and which he had commissioned some years previously. In all of this he was acting as a powerful catalyst, engaging the right people for the design and execution of the work and helping them to get on with the job. The great names, Henry Holland, John Nash, Sir John Soane and Jeffry Wyatt (later known as Wyatville) were the principal beneficiaries of his inspiration, but his encouragement and enthusiasm spread to everyone involved in the works, including the humblest craftsmen.

Once he had reached the Throne he had nothing to fear from those who were in a position to disclose the existence of his and Maria's secret marriage and family. One such person was Lady Hertford and his first action was to dismiss her from her privileged position as his consort.

It was wretched for him that his health was deteriorating so rapidly. It is possible that he started to suffer from his father's illness. In addition to his obesity, he developed dropsy which gave him a swollen face. This made him reluctant to be seen either by the public or his friends. He retired to Royal Lodge Windsor and apart from drives in the beautiful park, he seldom went elsewhere.

When Lord Liverpool died in 1827 he had difficulty finding a replacement for him. Eventually he appointed the Duke of Wellington who insisted on introducing Catholic Emancipation, a measure which he had promised Maria over forty years previously. The same year the Duke of York, the King's favourite brother, died, leaving the Duke of Clarence as his successor to the Throne.

In April 1830 he began to suffer a series of minor strokes. Maria wrote him an affectionate letter and had travelled to London from Brighton in case he wished to see her but he could not face emotional meetings. He died early in the morning of 26 June 1830.

The new King, William IV, who had always been friendly towards Maria as his brother's wife, remained a true friend to her as his brother's widow. He sent her a kind message and a few days after the funeral returned to her many of the jewels, trinkets and miniatures which from time to time she had given the late King. They were found in George IV's cabinet, but one tiny locket was missing and for this, a miniature of herself, Mrs Fitzherbert made particular inquiries.

It was not until some time later that the Duke of Wellington confessed to Minney that he had seen the miniature suspended around the King's neck at the time of his death and that it remained there to the end. In her house at Brighton the King's widow wept when she heard of this from their beloved daughter.

King William, Queen Adelaide and his illegitimate offspring made good use of the Royal Pavilion, treating it as a family home. They regarded their neighbour Maria as though she were a member of their family and gave her an open invitation to dine with them every night when they were in residence. William IV authorized Maria to wear widow's weeds and to adopt Royal livery for her servants. He offered to make her a Duchess[11] which she refused because her heir to the title would have to be declared and that would inevitably reveal the existence of her family.

Many of King William's daughters, who had inherited their actress mother's beauty, had made good marriages and their families were also made welcome by Queen Adelaide, who loved children; the Pavilion echoed to their eager chatter, piercing yells and merry laughter. One of the sailor King's favourite exercises was to pace up and down the Chain Pier as though he were back on the deck of one of the great ships of the line and in the town he happily mingled and conversed with the populace.

Compared to his pretty married daughters, King William's illegitimate sons were very badly placed. They were given the name Fitzclarence but no titles* or money. Maria's sons, thanks to her foresight in instigating the Family Trust, were far better off, not only were they legitimate but they were well provided for financially. They had all received their patrimony and on their father's death, although they could not benefit from his official will, they had received secret legacies from the Family Trust. It fell to George Payne to sell large tracts of land to raise the necessary funds. He had to disguise the need for these sales by fictitious extravagances and gambling losses.** It was at this time that he started extensive additions to Sulby Hall.[34]

Maria's promise to George, Prince of Wales forty-five years previously, when they embarked upon their wedding, was to keep the marriage secret as long as he lived. She was, therefore, released from her bond on his death. However, in view of his other official marriage to Princess Caroline, she determined to keep her secret and to seek her family's cooperation in doing so.†

---

* *Eventually, after repeated protests to their father, the eldest was created Earl of Munster and his brothers and sisters were given the rank of children of a Marquis.*

** *George Payne was reputed to have lost three fortunes inherited from unspecified relatives.*

† *In Payne family circles it has always been said that the continued but voluntary secrecy which they observed on the subject, was kept out of love, respect and loyalty to Mrs Fitzherbert.*

19

1830
Panic in Officialdom

Sir William Knighton had become one of the Regent's physicians in 1813 and the King's private secretary in 1822. He was a friend of Lady Conyngham who was plotting to replace Lady Hertford as his constant companion. In 1817, as executor to Sir John MacMahon, a previous secretary to the Regent, he came into possession of some letters from Mrs Fitzherbert.[35] He returned them to their rightful owner without comment. The King was so relieved that the papers had not gone astray that he promoted him to the additional positions of auditor to the Duchies of Cornwall and Lancaster. It was rumoured that his knowledge of this correspondence gave him a hold over his master, an allegation that is borne out by an experience Maria suffered from him at about the same time. Although a total stranger to Maria he called at her house in Brighton on the pretext of enquiring after her health, insisting on seeing her, and forced his way into her bedroom where she lay ill in bed. Maria was much alarmed, knowing what he was in search of.[36] She had him thrown out of her house and determined to have nothing more to do with the man. After that salutary warning she took care to remove her private papers to a place of safety.

She now found that Knighton, whom she knew of as a malignant courtier, was to act as one of the late King's executors, the other executor being the Duke of Wellington. These two men had access to all the private letters which the late King had received and kept during his lifetime, including those from Maria, from his children and from his children's official guardian in their early days, Jack Payne. They demanded of Mrs Fitzherbert that all corresponding letters of the late King's writing, addressed to her, should be handed over to them to examine, destroy or return. Maria had full confidence in the Duke of Wellington's unblemished honour but none in Sir William Knighton's honour, which she knew to be totally lacking.

Thanks to King William's influence it was agreed that all the correspondence in the executors' hands should be conveyed to Mrs Fitzherbert's London house. This was done in the presence of herself, the Duke of Wellington and Lord Albemarle[37] (but not Knighton) the letters from both sides were burnt,* with the exception of those letters and documents which she chose to keep.

The Duke's conduct was gentlemanly and friendly to Mrs Fitzherbert in every respect and she was perfectly satisfied. The parcel containing the papers which she chose to keep, was delivered to Coutts Bank where it would remain at the disposal of Lord Albemarle and Lord Stourton, a relative of hers.

Later, Lord Stourton suggested to Lord Albemarle that Mrs Fitzherbert should be asked to write on the back of her marriage certificate:

'No issue from this marriage.
Witness my hand. M. Fitzherbert'.

He offered this suggestion on two grounds: 'The first on historical grounds that in all after-times it may be known that there was no such issue; the second, that it will render the document more valuable and consequently more likely to be preserved'.

Lord Stourton wrote a draft** of this proposed endorse-

---

* *Lord Albemarle's son who assisted at this conflagration, wrote in his autobiography: '. . . some idea of the mass of manuscripts committed to the flames may be formed by an expression of the Duke to my father after several hours of burning: I think, my Lord, we had better hold our hand for a while or we shall set the old woman's chimney on fire'.*

The scorch marks on the mantelpiece remained until the house was demolished about a hundred years later.

** *This draft, unsigned, was found by Sir Shane Leslie in the*

ment and presented it to Mrs Fitzherbert for signature, but she smilingly objected to signing it 'on the score of delicacy'.

Leslie family papers.

The papers which Maria brought forward for George IV's executors were mainly those which had passed between herself and her husband. There was, of course, a huge amount of other correspondences which she continued to retain, probably spread amongst her many residences and ultimately lost. Some of this was found several years later by her confidant and executor, Sir George Seymour, including many early letters from the Prince to Jack Payne (who died in 1803). Sir George gave these to the Duke of Wellington for disposal. It was not known that he burned them but they have not been found again. Sir George commented, '. . . as far as I looked them over, though eloquent, they deserved the flames much better than preservation.' (Ragley Papers.)

In the prelude to his first book Mrs Fitzherbert *, Shane Leslie writes: 'But after all the precautions taken to destroy letters and abscond papers, it is almost a miracle for any biography to be possible. Research for material leads the gleaner from bonfire to bonfire. At times it has seemed useless to proceed . . . The most important correspondences have been gutted. Others have been ransacked and censored. Even notebooks have been scissored.' He describes how correspondences of other Royal lovers attracted no such attention, commenting – '. . . but in Mrs Fitzherbert's case serious account had to be taken. For she had crossed the sanctuary with her lover. . . For dynastic reasons her letters might become dynamic.'*

In his second book The Letters of Mrs Fitzherbert, *he writes in the introduction – '. . . Had her position been merely that of a discarded mistress, neither the* issue of her body *nor of her ink pot would have been considered dangerous.'*

20

1832-1841
Randolph Becomes Head of the Family

Two years after the King's death, Randolph's sixth son was born. He was named George in honour of Randolph's illustrious father who had always been so good to him.

In June 1834 the Reverend John Croft's sister had died and was buried under the high altar in St Peter's Church, Berkhamsted.[18] Early in 1836 John Croft stayed for a few days in Brighton with Maria.[38] He was now a very lonely man, having enjoyed his elder sister's companionship all his life. She had been seven years his senior. Randolph and his brothers continued to treat John Croft as a member of the Payne family and he extended his influence to the next generation as well.

In the last three years of her life, Maria had frequent discussions with her Roman Catholic cousin Lord Stourton, on the subject of her marriage and her married life. It was to him that she entrusted the vindication of her character with posterity. She authorized him to write her biography after her death and dictated to him sufficient of her life story which, together with the papers retained at Coutts Bank, she deemed to be adequate for her purpose. Unfortunately, she failed to fulfil his advice that she should write explicit instructions as to the disposition of her papers after the death of those she had appointed as her executors in regard to them.

Mrs Fitzherbert's enjoyment of her seventies continued into her eighties. She was always giving parties or circulating amongst her old friends and her seven children, including the five married couples who were continually adding to the number of her grandchildren.

The only change to her lifestyle was that she spent more time at Brighton than in London. In her eighty-first year she was making plans to travel abroad and to embark on some quite long trips in England.

There was no twilight period of her life. She was active to the end and her end came suddenly and quickly. She was taken ill, took to her bed and within a week, on 27 March 1837, she passed away. She was dead before Randolph and Frederick heard that she was ill. Marianne and Minney attended the funeral but the Paynes were there incognito, amongst the smart array of people admitted to St John the Baptist's Church, Brighton, by ticket only.

On 3 June, two and a half months later, King William IV died and Queen Victoria ascended the Throne at the tender age of eighteen.

The year of Maria's death, Randolph's wife Mary Anne gave birth to their seventh child (Randolph's eleventh). He wanted to call his new son Fitzherbert Payne, following his sister's example with her second son named 'Fitzherbert Edward Jerningham'; however, he decided that it would be imprudent to do so and the child was christened *Herbert* Payne at St Mary Abbot, Kensington. Randolph had become the head of the family; he and George Damer composed an obituary to Maria which was published in *The Brighton Gazette* on 30 March 1837. It was, of course, by mutual agreement attributed to George Damer. It read:

> THE LATE MRS FITZHERBERT.
>
> We have this day to announce the death of Mrs Fitzherbert.
>
> This distinguished lady has occupied too extraordinary a place in the history of the country, for her demise not to demand at our hands some tribute of respect and record.
>
> Those of our readers who will look back to some of the events that marked, in a very peculiar manner, the beginning of the latter half of the reign of George the Third, will remember the very interesting and remarkable position she then occupied in this country.
>
> Having avoided, by every means in her power, the position that afterwards became her lot, united by the

forms of her church to one who for many years had sought her; placed on an eminence whence she could do more injury, public and private, than anyone ever before her since the commencement of the last century; – by the effect of her personal charms, and the simplicity and integrity of her character, finding herself at the head of society, she thus, through a long life, succeeded in winning the respect of all those who were, by the circumstances of her situation, brought into contact with her; and when we say this, we mean that we have reason to believe that, from nearly the first moment her name became conspicuous in the annals of this country, she enjoyed the esteem and expressed regard of the very *highest personages* in it.

The influence she possessed was always exercised for the honour of the personage she was, by the forms of her church, united to. His honour, that of the country, and his position in it,were, it is well known, the first objects of her anxiety.

Through an existence prolonged beyond the lot of most people, she made more real friends than almost any one that we are acquainted with. Those friendships were cemented by a reliance on the integrity of her character, and led to unlimited confidence, which was ever observed by her with sacred inviolability. The honour, frankness, and straightforwardness of her disposition, procured her the intimate acquaintance of some of the most eminent men of the times in which she lived; and many of them are still alive, and can bear witness to the truth and fidelity with which this portrait of her is drawn, and to the affectionate respect with which, to her latest breath, they have continued to regard her.

In her more familiar circle she was generous, indulgent, and hospitable. She retained in advanced age the warmth, the enthusiasm, the freshness and disinterested feelings of youth. Her piety was fervent and unostentatious. Her life was one of active benevolence. Her cheerfulness was very remarkable, and evidently the result of the pleasure she was herself afforded by making others happy.

Many are those who have been the objects of her

> generosity to a very unusual degree. Charity was never asked of her in vain. Very numerous are the persons who for years have existed on her support.
>
> To her more immediate attendants, she was at once a friend and a benefactress.
>
> She has sunk into the grave, full of years, having a firm reliance on the merits of our Saviour, lamented by all who had the happiness to know her, but deeply deplored by those who for many years have been the objects upon whom her tender solicitude was lavished, and who will ever revere her memory.
>
> Her loss to the poor will be irreparable; and society in general will feel the void left by one who possessed, in an eminent degree, more of the finer qualities of our nature, and fewer of the imperfect, than any one to whom we can at present allude.
>
> We shall close this hasty and incomplete sketch of the character of this most excellent and exalted lady, by informing our readers that she was one of the first persons who attracted good company to Brighton, and to her, undoubtedly, were due many of the first advantages possessed by this town.
>
> Mrs Fitzherbert departed this life on Monday last, the 27th, at seven in the evening, in the 81st year of her age.

Maria, like her husband, had been unable to mention her secret children in her will and once again they were provided for from the Payne family Trust. On this occasion the Trust was wound up and the amount each received was an equal share of its residual assets which were in the region of £20,000 each. As before, to camouflage the huge sales of land in the shires, George Payne of Sulby Hall feigned to have incurred enormous gambling losses. This was the third fortune he was reputed to have lost in racing and gambling. In total, enough to build a battleship!

Back in 1830, when Randolph received his first legacy he moved to numbers 32/33 Kensington Square, a most prestigious residence near to Kensington Palace.[39] When he received this second legacy he purchased 61 St James's Street,[40] Piccadilly, as his business headquarters. He had a Deed of Partnership drawn up for the family business which became 'Randolph Payne and Son'. These Deeds of Partnership, making his eldest son Randolph his first partner, were signed on Christmas Day 1838, when he was twenty-four years of age.

The Crofts had given all of Randolph's children a good grounding in the Anglican faith while Maria had introduced them to the more colourful ritual of the Roman Catholic Mass. To these five boys and girls, Maria was the most perfect Christian and yet she was of a different religious faith from theirs; a faith which was discriminated against by other Christians. This seemed to them to be entirely wrong and as a result they all had a marked sympathy for the Roman Catholic Church. Young Randolph had a strong inclination to take Holy Orders.

William Payne, his younger brother, was nineteen at the time and was learning the business by operating on a commission basis from The Carlton Hotel in Regent Street.[41] Like their father and their uncles, because Randolph and William knew their own impeccable social rank, they were able to conduct valuable business in the highest and the lowest strata of society, without the slightest inhibitions or embarrassment from either side and they often mixed business with pleasure. Both young men had been to Tours to learn that side of the trade and William in particular had developed a very good palate and judgment of wines.[42]

On the subject of their father's connection with Maria and King George IV, Randolph's own children were the height of discretion but when the three eldest daughters married into the Geare, the Wix and the Goss families, the in-laws were quite naturally interested in their antecedents.* There was no wish to be evasive over the subject, the problem was how to keep the information within the ever-growing circle of confidants. Despite this difficulty the secret was very well

---

* *It is passed down through the generations that if Randolph was pressed on the subject he would say, 'my parents were respectably married and I was the rightful heir to the Throne at my father's death'.*

kept.

An example of this discretion is manifest in the wording on Maria's memorial. This was commissioned and placed in St John the Baptist's Church where she had been buried. It was carved by Carew, a protégé of Lord Egremont. The wording on the commemorative plaque reads:

> '. . . one to whom she was more than a parent
> has placed this monument. . .'

It would have been a costly work and her other children would have wanted to contribute even if their contribution could not be declared. To them such a restraint was their normal obligation. By mutual consent their youngest sister Minney represented them all.

Many years later, three sons of Frederick Wyndham Payne, Randolph, Frank and William, who had emigrated to the USA, returned as American tourists to Maria's shrine. They met the priest, Monsignor Johnson, at the Church and told him that they were Mrs Fitzherbert's descendants and that their forbears had placed this monument to her memory. He was so astounded by their claim that he immediately reported it to Lady Constance Leslie, Minney's surviving daughter.

The year after Maria's death there was an article in *The Edinburgh Review* on her marriage to the Prince of Wales which contained errors of fact and a letter from Lord Stourton, correcting these errors, was published in the following number of the journal. In 1841 he made an attempt to get access to the papers in Coutts Bank but the Duke of Wellington declined to give his consent.*

---

* *Lord Stourton continued his attempts to get access to Maria's papers but died before he could do so. He delegated the responsibilities he had undertaken on Maria's behalf to his brother, the Hon Charles Langdale who published his book,* Memoirs of Mrs Fitzherbert, *in 1856. Subsequent biographies were written by W H Wilkins, Sir Shane Leslie and others.*

This book covers the period up to the end of the nineteenth century. The saga of Maria's secret papers dragged on into the twentieth century and they are now amongst the private archives of the Royal Family at Windsor Castle. A fuller account of their fate is given in an appendix.

21

1842-1862
The Sands Run Out for Randolph

The era in which Randolph and his children lived was the most exciting in human history. Since the dawn of the human race, transport on land had been limited to the speed and strength of men and animals, while on the oceans it was limited to the strength of manpower and the uncertainty of the winds. In this era steam-power with its vastly greater potential for speed and load was progressively introduced; means of connecting heat to motive power had been discovered, with profound effect on the future. Steam power on the oceans was in the lead because water could take the new type of traffic right away; steam-driven paddle-ships had been used at the beginning of the century for short distances. It was closely followed on land once a new type of roadway, which the French so aptly named *le chemin de fer*, was invented (by the British). With 'steel rail' roads and steam locomotives the age of the railway train began.

Maria herself had seen one of the earliest railways, the Liverpool to Manchester line, under construction during a visit to Sir Thomas Stanley at Hooton,* but she never travelled on a steam-train, nor saw one in action. The London, Brighton and South Coast Railway Company was formed in the year of Maria's death. 'Railway mania' started in Britain in 1844 and lines spread all over the country, while sailing ships were giving way to steam at an accelerating pace.

Suburban railways were changing people's lives by opening

---

* *Sir Thomas Stanley married Maria's niece Mary Haggerston. Frederick Wyndham Payne named one of his sons 'Harry Stanley'.*

up towns and villages like Kingston, Walton-on-Thames and Molesey as residential areas from which gentlemen travelled daily to central London and back. Photography was invented. Gas light was replacing candles. Electric telegraphic communication started and its potential was developed as rapidly as steam-power. However, it was a long time before mechanical power replaced the horse on the streets and highways of town and country. A man could travel from New York to Southampton in a steam-propelled passenger ship and then to London on a fast and comfortable train, having a four course meal as he went, but from Waterloo Station to his house in Mayfair he was dragged through the streets by an animal, albeit a noble one!

These developments affected the latter part of Randolph's life. He and Mary Anne could travel in comfort and quickly from London to Brighton and even across the Channel to Tours.

Back in 1842, Randolph Junior decided to go into the Church. His brother William replaced him as a partner in Randolph Payne and Son and his half-brother Frederick Wyndham entered the firm. Randolph Junior went to Magdalen Hall, Oxford,[43] graduating in 1846. As soon as he was ordained, he chose to return to Brighton, the scene of much of his early life, as a Deacon of the Parish Church of St Nicholas. The Clergy of this parish served other Churches and for several years his responsibilities included the parish of Wiston,[43] a small hamlet ten miles from Brighton. He enjoyed riding there and back across the South Downs on his own horse. He became one of the first curates of St Paul's in Brighton,* a newly-built church completed in 1848. St Paul's was 'high church', displaying a more elaborate ritual than was usual in Anglican churches and attracted huge congregations because it compared so favourably with the strict puritanical

---

* *Randolph Junior never married and remained a curate at St Paul's, Brighton for the rest of his life, living in the family home.*

Twenty years later, Randolph's youngest son, Alfred, also went into the Church and started his Ministry as curate-in-charge of St Bartholomew's Church, Brighton. Like his elder brother, he too, was 'high church'. He married Julia Maria Brownlow, a member of the great family.[43]

attitudes of the day, when such embellishments as a surpliced choir or the chanting of psalms were considered Popish.[44] Randolph Senior bought 7 Norfolk Terrace in Brighton[45] both for his family's visits to the town, which became more and more frequent, for his Clergyman son and in anticipation of his own retirement.

When Queen Victoria succeeded to the Throne in 1837 she spent six weeks in the autumn at the Pavilion. She did not like the place very much and returned there very infrequently. The following year she disembarked the the Royal Yacht at the Chain Pier after a visit to King Louis Philippe in Normandy and left a week later, again from the Pier, to visit her uncle, King Leopold of the Belgians (Princess Charlotte's widower). In February 1845, she travelled to Brighton in the Royal Train but she, Prince Albert, and four of their children, were irritated by the attentions of the huge crowd of 'trippers' who had also made use of the new railway. That was her last visit to the Pavilion. Soon afterwards Prince Albert bought Osborne House on the Isle of Wight, which gave them much more privacy. The Pavilion as a Royal home had become redundant.

The following year a start was made on stripping the Pavilion of all its fine furniture and decorations for use in Buckingham Palace and Windsor Castle.* By 1848 it was an empty shell awaiting demolition with a view to selling the site for property development. The people of Brighton were most dismayed and made successful overtures to stop the demolition. In 1850, the town commissioners bought and took possession of the property, paying £53,000.

In 1842, William had married Maria Damant, who came from an old Huguenot family, connected with Archbishop Sancroft. William and Maria had a big society wedding at St James's, Westminster, and took over Randolph's house in Kensington Square while he moved to Highbury House on

---

* *Since then furniture and ornaments, not used in other palaces, have been progressively returned to the building, a process which continues to this day.*

WILLIAM PAYNE.
A painting by Lillian Payne.

Lavender Hill (near to Sherwood Lodge) which remained in the Payne family possession for many years.

A proud moment for Randolph was William's appointment as 'Gentleman of Her Majesty's Wine Cellars', in February 1859.[46] William was granted apartments in St James's Palace by the Lord Chamberlain. He was conveniently close to 61 St

James's Street, the headquarters of the family firm.* As a member of Queen Victoria's Household, he had to give up his partnership in the family wine business and he handed over both his partnership and his Kensington Square house to his half-brother, Frederick Wyndham. William moved his household to Molesey near Hampton Court. From there he could travel to London and back by train.

In 1862 Randolph, 'the first Mr Payne' died, at the age of seventy-two, at his home in Brighton as his mother Maria had done. In his will he left instructions that his funeral should be conducted without pomp and with strict regard to economy.

His special bequests included:

> To his wife, Mary Anne, the last two portraits of himself and of her painted by Henry Room.
>
> A miniature portrait of himself painted when he was only twenty-one, to his son, Randolph.
>
> A silver watch that had belonged to his brother William Payne, to his son, William.
>
> The miniature of his late mother** and a miniature portrait of his late brother William to his daughter, Julia.
>
> His silver watch that had belonged to his brother Frederick, to his nephew, Randolph (Frederick's son).

Thus, with humility and dignity Randolph of the House of Guelph (alias Payne) eldest legitimate son of a reigning English Monarch and of his wife Maria, who was one of the most outstanding Englishwomen of her time, passed away unrecognized in the annals of English history.

---

* *It is Payne family tradition that the cellars of 61 St James's Street joined the cellars of St James's Palace.*

** *The whereabouts of this portrait of Maria is unknown today.*

22

1862-1896
The Second Bonfire

Randolph outlived all his brothers and sisters, except for the youngest, George. He left 9/16th share of the family business to his son Frederick Wyndham and the remainder to his son Charles. Frederick Wyndham took charge of the wine business and continued to give lucrative jobs to any members of the Payne family who wanted to work with him. Randolph Payne and Son's clients included the Royal Family and all ranks of nobility and gentlemen all over the country who had large cellars to stock and entertained on a grand scale. Sales were made largely by personal contact and depended on the recommendation of the supplier and his personal reputation for taste,* judgment and honesty. The Paynes had an enormous clientele in these social circles with whom they mixed on easy and friendly terms. That was their strength in those days and was to remain so for many years to come. Although William was no longer in the firm, his Royal Household appointment gave its reputation a great boost. He was also Gentleman of the Prince of Wales' Wine Cellars.

William was leading a very good life; he got on extremely well with the Queen and with other courtiers; he regularly visited the Royal palaces including Balmoral in Scotland and Osborne in the Isle of Wight and he had a special passport for use when travelling abroad on Her Majesty's business. He was very public-spirited and became a Churchwarden of the Parish of St Mary's, Molesey; he contributed to the building of

* *The 'Payne Papers' include numerous personal letters expressing appreciation of the consignments provided.*

ALEXANDER PAYNE
(William Payne's Son)
Twice winner of The Wingfield Sculls.

a new aisle for the Church and his name as Churchwarden is carved on the foundation stone of the aisle together with that of his friend, Lady Sarah Spencer who laid the stone in 1883. He changed houses in Molesey several times over the years, naming one of his residences Redbourn House after his birthplace, and another Croft House after the Reverend John Croft whom Maria had employed as tutor to the Payne family.

Life was also good for William's two daughters and five

sons. They all lived in the charming village of Molesey near Hampton Court on the River Thames. They were extremely well-off and were surrounded by good friends including their great-aunts, the Misses New. William's five sons were light-hearted, athletic, pleasure-seeking and wild. The River Thames was their playground and they loved all aquatic sports, particularly rowing. They were founder-members of the Molesey Boat Club and at one time the five brothers crewed a rowing four with the youngest as cox, competing in all the regattas up and down the river. One of the brothers, Alex Payne, was amongst the most famous rowing men of the day, having won the 'Wingfield Sculls' twice. This was the race for single sculls over the University Boat Race course from Putney to Mortlake. He also excelled at long distance skating on the Fens.

They all played 'real tennis' at Hampton Court with the Prince of Wales and his brothers. They had a private fire-engine and, wearing their firemen's helmets, rushed off to fires in the district, brass polished, horses' hooves pounding and bells clanging. During the great freeze of 1878/79* Alex, for a bet, drove up the frozen Thames from London Bridge to Hampton Court in a coach and four. He worked at 61 St James's Street where his uncle was training him in clerical work and in developing his taste and judgment of wine. He also took over his father's contacts, who would call on him to enjoy his company in drinking, gambling and indulging in the club and night life of the big city. His pay-off was when these friends placed big orders to replenish their cellars or for some large social occasion. As they bought their suits in Savile Row and their hats in Bond Street, they ordered their wine from Randolph Payne and Son in St James's Street and took the young Paynes out on the spree in the process.

Edward, Prince of Wales, and his brothers were kindred spirits; they were all playboys together. There was a remarkable likeness between William's sons and the young Princes. They were often mistaken for Royalty in the streets, when passers-by raised their hats to them. On one occasion William

---

* *The great freeze-up lasted from October to May and many cricket matches were played on the ice throughout the winter* (Wisden Anthology 1864-1900).

and one of his sons were descending a staircase in the palace when they saw the Queen approaching. They made way for her respectfully and as she passed she turned to the young man and said, 'Arthur, I thought you told me that you would be out of London today.' She mistook William's son for her own son, Prince Arthur of Connaught![46]

It was a great tragedy for the whole family when William's eldest son and heir, Reginald (Rex), died of typhoid fever at the age of twenty-five in 1869. His parents put up a memorial window to him in the new aisle of St Mary's Church, Molesey.

In due course, all of William's other sons and daughters married except for Guybon, the youngest, and set up homes of their own. The apartments in St James's Palace were a great asset to William's family. They could all use them when they were in London and when they went to the theatre or to the opera they could stay there for the night. If their father were with them, the band would play any tune they chose at his request.

In April 1884, Alex married Lillian Louisa Drury, the attractive and talented daughter of the Venerable Archdeacon Drury. The wedding took place at the Parish Church of Wraxall, Somerset, with three high-ranking clergymen officiating. In their early married life they lived on a large houseboat on the Thames near Molesey but later they moved to Heath House* in St Albans, which they rented from Lord Spencer who had an estate between St Albans and Wheathampstead.[47] The railway had reached St Albans many years earlier.

Alex and his wife took a great interest in the new Church called St Saviours which was being built at that time. It was to be 'High Church', using ritual in its services, for which they shared the strong family preference.

Alex was a rich young man but he was also generous to a fault. He was always lending money, backing his friends' loans and guaranteeing their bank overdrafts. The Prince of Wales, who was always short of money, borrowed from Alex and also

---

* *Heath House, on the Harpenden Road, exists today. In Alex's day, it was the last house in the town. It was very close to Redbourn, his father's birthplace.*

from William. Sometimes the sums involved were more than either of them could raise so, very foolishly, Alex found financiers for him and guaranteed his loans. Meanwhile, they were supplying him with large quantities of wine for which he did not pay. In 1886, Alex endeavoured to get payment, at least for the wines he had supplied over the last few years, but was told 'HRH has never paid *any* invoices yet and we do not like to claim.'[46]

After 1880, William had some costly commitments in connection with two of his other sons and his financial situation was considerably reduced. In 1882 he wrote to Sir Henry Ponsonby, the Queen's Private Secretary, to ask whether he could, in a year or so, retire on his pension in favour of his son Alex. The reply was not encouraging and confirmed that the appointment was not hereditary. In 1888, when he was approaching the age of seventy, he wrote a private letter from his home, Redbourn House, Molesey, to Sir John Cowell, Master of the Household, [42]referring back to his letter on the subject six years previously. William wrote: '. . .*I trained him* (Alex) *for many years previously* in clerical work, and specially in *tasting.* I can truly say that with regard to his taste that it is very correct and consistent – in fact as good as my own. I hope I am not showing any conceit in making such a statement, but you are judge how far, generally, my taste is correct, as well as others in the Royal Household. During the last four years he has been working with his brother – not as a Partner, but selling Wine on Commission. I thought this would be doing him more good, than keeping him *solely* to help *me.*' The reply was non-committal, but Sir John minuted on William's letter, 'I would today warmly support the appointment of Mr Payne's son as his successor, if the position was vacant.'

One of the Prince's debts, repayment of which Alex had guaranteed, was to a German Jew called Herr Schomberg. When this moneylender failed to get satisfaction from the Prince of Wales he took Alex up on his guarantee and sued him for repayment. Alex in desperation sued the Prince, a quite unprecedented step. This caused an uproar in Court and came to the notice of the Queen. Somehow in the course of the ensuing row the Payne family connection with Mrs Fitzherbert came out into the open. It is most likely that it was

Edward, Prince of Wales who betrayed them, knowing that her shock and indignation on hearing this disclosure would distract his mother's attention from his own indiscretion.

Alex received no sympathy for the financial predicament into which his generosity towards the Queen's eldest son had led him; her only concern was the Payne connection with Mrs Fitzherbert. She had no knowledge of the policy of extreme discretion which the Payne family exercised over the subject. 'This' she declared, 'is information which no loyal subject should wish to possess'[48] and demanded the surrender of all documentary evidence which supported the facts.

Yet another bonfire was lit and completed the destruction by the Duke of Wellington's great conflagration in Maria's drawing-room fireplace fifty years before. It consumed documents which had previously escaped the flames or were of subsequent origin. William and Alex were sworn to secrecy on the subject, but there was still plenty of memory which was not imprisoned by a vow. It is significant that at that time, Lady Constance Leslie, Minney Seymour's youngest daughter, (and William Payne's first cousin) was busy with scissors cutting out from her collection of family papers all reference to Maria's children.[49] She had, no doubt, heard of the fate of William Payne and his cherished family documents.

Alex was bankrupted and in supporting his son so also was William. Both had to sell everything they possessed to fulfil their guarantee. All the trophies of Alex's sporting achievements were photographed and sold. He spent the rest of his life trying, with little success, to turn his enterprise and energies into money. William resigned from his office in the Prince's Household but continued to serve the Queen until he retired in 1892. Having been a rich man, he moved into a small terraced house near Clapham Common, living on the £50 a year which was all that a bankrupt was allowed by court to keep for himself. He died without money or possessions in 1896.

The family's downfall stemmed from the fateful day in 1859 when William accepted his appointment in the Royal Household as 'Gentleman of the Wine Cellars' to the Queen and later to the Prince of Wales. This kept them enmeshed in Court circles from which they should have stayed aloof and minded their own flourishing family business. The wine business degenerated into a family trust fund providing annuities for the widows and spinsters. When Randolph's youngest daughter, Augusta, died in Brighton in 1947 at the age of one hundred, the business 'Randolph Payne and Son' founded one hundred and nine years before by Maria Fitzherbert's eldest son, ceased to exist.

EPILOGUE

The story of Maria's secret marriage was sufficiently well-known in her lifetime to generate a large number of claims by individuals (not families) to be her offspring. These were normally based on the supposition that the parents had discarded their new-born babies as though they were an unimportant by-product of their romance and claimants thought themselves to be the survivors of such heartless action. Maria Fitzherbert was a woman who was not only beautiful in looks and charm but had the strictest of moral and Christian principles and the kindest of hearts. If there were women who would stoop to such tyranny, Maria was the least likely to be amongst them. The fact that the Payne family made no such claims but by contrast kept their bond of secrecy out of loyalty to the Crown and out of loving respect for their matriarch, Maria Fitzherbert, is itself testimony to the truth of their origin.

If any documentary evidence had survived, to substantiate the fact that George and Maria had a secret family by their marriage, there would be no mystery to unravel. The fact that the authorities went to such frantic measures to seek out and destroy every scrap of documentary evidence that could be traced is strong circumstantial evidence supporting the truth.

Family history should not be disrespected. Consider that your grandparent discussed your family history with you when you were ten years of age; you could carry that information quite accurately in your head for the rest of your life. Then, consider that you passed that information on to your ten-year old grandchild; he could carry this information in his head for the remainder of his life. Just those two spans of personal memory, your grandparent to yourself and yourself to your grandchild, cover the span of time between Randolph Payne's life and his descendants still alive today; or the span of time between Maria's life and the generation just departed.

Three of the most significant points of family history were the facts that Admiral Jack Payne became the children's guardian; that they took his surname and that they were given jobs in Court when their education was completed. It is well known that while the Prince and Maria were living in matrimonial bliss, Admiral Jack Payne was the Prince of Wales' great friend, confidant, private secretary and Comptroller of his Household, while the Admiral enjoyed a similar friendship and mutual confidence with Maria.

Added to that, there were numerous other disparate items of circumstantial evidence (extending over three generations) which fit the hypothesis. This book has set out the enormous accumulation of such evidence into a continuous narrative; all the evidence is lifted from recorded and accepted history. Furthermore, the hypothesis gains strength from the inadequacy of all other possible explanations of the mystery.

Why did this healthy young and passionate couple, who lived as man and wife for twenty years, to whom no birth control was possible and when each had produced children by other marriages, have no children of their own union? George and Princess Caroline had a daughter; Maria and Thomas Fitzherbert had a son. Why was the birth of this son, born before Maria's marriage to George, kept so secret? Why did Maria refuse to deny that she and George had issue from their union? Why did Maria decline William IV's offer to make her a Duchess, a title that would have required her to declare any legitimate male heirs?

Why does Randolph Payne's baptism certificate give, as his parents, people whose existence cannot be found in any other public records of their time and why could not this well-educated and well-endowed young man declare the identity of his mother and father to those outside his family circles?

If Randolph and his brothers and sisters had been the children of George by any other woman there would have been no need for a false name nor for any secrecy as to their parentage; furthermore, they would probably have been given titles and retained noble rank. In their determination to respect their mother's wish that they should not disclose their identity, it was *her* name that was the vital secret; if her name had once been revealed as the parent of legitimate Protestant children, their innocent private secret would have become an instant source of acute embarrassment to them. It could even have led to their social and financial ruin. Maria's grandson, William Payne, and his son Alex, learned this to their cost when the truth came to the ears of Queen Victoria.

APPENDIX

The Saga of Mrs Fitzherbert's Secret Papers

This appendix is based on extracts from the biographies of Mrs Fitzherbert written by W H Wilkins, the historian of the House of Hanover, in 1905 and by Sir Shane Leslie, one of Minney's descendants, in 1940. They show, in very great detail, the extraordinary importance which first the Duke of Wellington and later King Edward VII attached to the continued secrecy of these papers, long after Maria's valid marriage to the Prince of Wales in 1785 had been accepted as an historical fact and had become public knowledge.

This book has included two 'bonfires' fuelled by Maria's secret papers; the reader may detect a third bonfire, a smaller but highly selective one. Once the papers had been removed from the security of the Bank and once they had fallen into the hands of persons unsympathetic to Maria's intentions, and once the seal had been broken, the removal of some of the papers would never be noticed.

All quotations in Part I of this appendix are from Langdale's *Memoir,* unless otherwise stated.

I. FROM W H WILKINS:

When in August 1833 Mrs Fitzherbert placed the papers which she had reserved from the burning at Coutts Bank, 'at the disposal of the Earl of Albemarle and Lord Stourton,' it was to Lord Stourton that she looked chiefly for help and guidance concerning them. Lord Stourton was her cousin and a Roman Catholic. Necessarily, therefore, there existed between them a community of interest which could not be shared by Lord Albemarle, who though a trusted friend, was bound to her by neither the tie of blood nor of religion. It was necessary for Mrs Fitzherbert to have two trustees, but it was to Lord Stourton that she entrusted the vindication of her character with posterity. This is clear from a letter she wrote to him from Paris, December 7, 1833, a few months after the papers had been deposited at Coutts Bank. After thanking him for the interest he took in her affairs, she said:

'I know I must have been a great torment to you, but I am sure the kind feelings of your heart will derive some gratification, in having relieved me from a state of misery and anxiety which has been the bane of my life, and *I trust, whenever it shall please God to remove me from this world, my conduct and character (in your hands) will not disgrace my family and my friends.*'

Mrs Fitzherbert's intention, therefore, with regard to the papers was perfectly clear. On her return to England in 1834, and during the last three years of her life (1834-1837), she frequently discussed the subject with Lord Stourton. She authorized him to write her biography after her death, and dictated a short narrative of her life to him, which, with the papers she had retained at Coutts Bank, she deemed sufficient for the purpose. The time she left to his discretion. Lord Stourton urged her to give more definite instructions as to what was to be done with the papers in the case of the death of one or both of the trustees, and she promised to do so, but postponed the matter. After the death of Sir William Knighton in 1836, Lord Stourton again raised the question. He wrote to her (November 19, 1836): 'What disposition of these papers is to be made, *after the demise of those* whom you have appointed executors in regard of them?'* and asking for more explicit instructions. Mrs Fitzherbert merely acknowledged Lord Stourton's letter, and promised to discuss the matter fully with him when she next came to London.

It is unwise to delay when one is over eighty; and a few months after writing this letter Mrs Fitzherbert died, without leaving any definite instructions as to what was to be done with the papers at Coutts Bank. Hence arose the difficulties and confusion that followed. Some ten days after Mrs Fitzherbert's death, in consequence of the announcement of an

---

* *Extract from a letter of Lord Stourton's to Mrs Fitzherbert at Brighton, dated Allerton, November 29, 1836.*

unauthorized memoir, Lord Albemarle wrote to Lord Stourton (April 6, 1837) and suggested that they should consult together concerning 'the charge confided to us.' The publication of the unauthorized memoir was presumably prevented, since none appeared, and Lord Stourton, to whom the task of writing the authorized biography had been entrusted by Mrs Fitzherbert, wished to break the seals of the package at Coutts Bank to see what was in the papers. But the Duke of Wellington's *knowledge* was necessary to the opening of the parcel: the Duke considered this also to mean his *consent*, and he demurred. Lord Albemarle did not like to press the matter in the face of the Duke's unwillingness, and so Lord Stourton was reluctantly induced to yield to the Duke's suggestion that the documents should be left, for the time, undisturbed.

Though foiled in this instance, Lord Stourton continued to keep watch over Mrs Fitzherbert's good name and fair memory. In 1838, there appeared in the *Edinburgh Review** an article on the marriage of Mrs Fitzherbert to the Prince of Wales, which, though favourable to the deceased lady, contained certain errors of fact. Lord Stourton at once wrote to correct these errors. His letter was inserted in the following number of the *Edinburgh Review** and contained the following: 'The marriage ceremony was performed not out of the kingdom, as you have stated, but in her own drawing-room, in her house in town, in the presence of an officiating Protestant clergyman, and of two of her own nearest relatives.'

One would have thought this statement was conclusive coming as it did from one of the leading Roman Catholic laymen in England, a cousin and trustee of the deceased lady. But the public denials in the House of Commons of Mrs Fitzherbert's marriage were not forgotten, and it was still regarded as an open question whether she had been through any ceremony of marriage with the late King George IV. No one was more conscious of this than Lord Stourton, and in 1841 he made another attempt to have the packet at Coutts Bank opened, and so put all doubt to an end. 'The first question is,' he wrote to Lord Albemarle, 'and to that I cannot reply in any way satisfactorily myself, what these papers are?'

---

* *Edinburgh Review, No. CXXXV/VI*

He asked Lord Albemarle to see the Duke of Wellington about it. Lord Albemarle did so, and wrote to Lord Stourton (February 1, 1841) a letter in which he said that he had called upon the Duke, who read Lord Stourton's letter. 'He then requested me to state to you, that he felt he had a public duty as well as a private one to perform in keeping the papers alluded to, if possible, undisturbed, on account of their importance: that there was not now, nor had there been, any attack upon Mrs Fitzherbert's reputation. Did any appear in any quarter, he would be eager in joining us to repel it.' The Duke, however, expressed his willingness to discuss the matter with Lord Stourton, when he should come to town.

Lord Stourton heard nothing further from the Duke until he received a long letter, dated 'Walmer Castle, August 10, 1841,' in which, after stating his view of the circumstances which led to the placing of the papers in Coutts Bank, the Duke said:

'Circumstances have in some degree changed since the death of Mrs Fitzherbert, but it is still very desirable to avoid drawing public attention to, and re-awakening, the subject by public discussion of the narrations to which the papers relate, which are deposited in the packet sealed up, to which I have above referred. And I am convinced that neither I nor any of the survivors of the royal family, of those who lived in the days in which these transactions occurred, could view with more pain any publication or discussion of them than would the late Mrs Fitzherbert when alive. Under these circumstances, and having acted conscientiously and upon honour throughout the affairs detailed in this letter, I cannot but consider it my duty to protest, and I do protest most solemnly, against the measure proposed by your Lordship, that of breaking the seals affixed to the packet of papers belonging to the late Mrs Fitzherbert, deposited at Messrs Coutts, the bankers, under the several seals of the Earl of Albemarle, your Lordship, and myself.'

Nothing daunted by the Duke's decided tone, Lord Stourton again in April 1842 made a last attempt to see these papers, and asked the Duke to give him an interview with Lord Albemarle. But the Duke, though he did not decline the meeting, postponed it indefinitely. Lord Stourton was later in this year taken seriously ill, and became a confirmed invalid. On December 22, 1842, he told his brother, Mr Charles Langdale, of the trust Mrs Fitzherbert had confided in him, and of the position in which he was placed with regard to the papers she had placed at Coutts Bank to vindicate her memory. As his ill-health made it impossible for him to fulfil the trust, he solemnly committed it to his brother. Lord Stourton died on December 4, 1846, and all the correspondence and papers which he had collected on the subject, together with the narrative dictated to him by Mrs Fitzherbert, were placed in the hands of Mr Langdale for the purpose of writing a biography. Lord Stourton also willed to his brother his share of control over the papers at Coutts Bank. This he had no legal power to do, as by his death they fell under the control of Lord Albemarle, the surviving trustee. Mr Langdale, however, formally applied to Messrs Coutts to see the papers, and as he had no legal status, his request was formally refused. He then wrote to Lord Albemarle and the Duke of Wellington, informing them of his brother's wishes, and he received a promise from them that the documents should not be removed from Coutts Bank without informing him. Lord Albemarle died in 1851, and his trusteeship of Mrs Fitzherbert's papers passed to his brother, the Rev. the Hon. E.S.Keppel, whom he made his executor. The Duke of Wellington died in 1852.

Mr Langdale, uncertain how to proceed, suffered the matter to rest until 1854, when the publication of Lord Holland's posthumous 'Memoirs of the Whig Party' revived the question anew. In these 'Memoirs' Lord Holland referred to the marriage of the Prince of Wales to Mrs Fitzherbert, and said:

'The exact date and circumstances of that ceremony have not come to my knowledge; but the account given of some part of the transaction by Mrs Fitzherbert herself to a friend of mine, a man of strict veracity, is curious, and I believe correct. It was at the Prince's own earnest and repeated solicitations, and not at Mrs Fitzherbert's request, that any ceremony was resorted to. She knew it to be invalid in law; she thought it nonsense, and told the Prince so. In proof that such had been her uniform opinion, she adduced a very striking circumstance, namely – that no ceremony by a Roman Catholic priest took place at all; the most obvious method of allaying her scruples, had she had any. I believe, therefore, that she spoke with truth when she frankly owned that she had given herself up to him, exacted no conditions, trusted to his honour, and set no value on the ceremony which he insisted on having solemnized.'*

Mr Langdale regarded this as an attack on Mrs Fitzherbert's honour and good faith, and a reflection on her religion, as her marriage was regarded as valid by her Church. He thought that the time had come for him to write Mrs Fitzherbert's biography, and tell the true story of the marriage. He therefore wrote to Mr Edward Keppel (November 16, 1854), and requested that 'a copy of the preserved documents should be placed at my disposal, the more effectively to establish the grounds upon which the friends and relations of this Lady have ever maintained her full and fair claim to their respect and esteem, and to the character of an honourable and religious woman.'

In reply Mr Keppel asked for time to consider the matter, and informed Mr Langdale, 'The packet you refer to is safe at Coutts', the seals at present unbroken.'

Mr Langdale agreed to a few weeks' delay only, premising 'that it is important the defence should not be too long delayed.' Months passed and he heard nothing. He therefore wrote again, February 16, 1855, asking for a definite answer. Then Mr Keppel wrote, February 23, 1855, and said that he had consulted the Duke of Bedford, and through him taken the opinion of Mrs Fitzherbert's surviving executors, Sir George Seymour and Mr Forster. 'They are strongly against the production of these papers. They would only prove the marriage of the Prince with Mrs Fitzherbert, which is not questioned, as Lord Holland's remarks go to the motives and feelings of her herself and the Prince, which the evidence in the papers would not touch.'

Against this decision, Mr Langdale lodged a spirited protest, and announced his intention of defending Mrs Fitzherbert's reputation at all costs. He reminded Mr Keppel

* 'Memoirs of the Whig Party, *by Lord Holland, edited by his son. Vol ii, p.140.*

that the papers were placed in Coutts Bank by Mrs Fitzherbert to prove her marriage with the Prince of Wales, and that was the only reason they were placed there. He added: 'That the reserved papers were intended for such a purpose, and that the trustees to whose charge they were committed received them with such an understanding from her whose property they were, you must excuse me if I confidently repeat. The refusal to place them at my disposal, renders it more imperative upon me to lay before the public the whole detail of the connection between Mrs Fitzherbert and George IV, then Prince of Wales, as narrated by herself to the late Lord Stourton; and which, without the reserved documents, will, I trust, show to the world, that whatever the conduct of George IV may have been, that of Mrs Fitzherbert, under trials of no ordinary description, was such as to have done honour to the purity of her character as a woman, and to her principles as a Catholic.'

Mr Langdale thereupon wrote the 'Memoirs of Mrs Fitzherbert, with an account of her Marriage with HRH the Prince of Wales, afterwards King George the Fourth,'* to which frequent reference has been made in this book. The book consists of the short narrative of her life which Mrs Fitzherbert told to Lord Stourton; a list of the papers which she had deposited at Coutts Bank, and all the correspondence which had passed relating to them after her death. Mr Langdale made an eloquent defence of Mrs Fitzherbert as a woman of virtue and a good Roman Catholic. He thus defends his own action in publishing the book:

'All minor considerations,' he says, 'must yield before the paramount duty to the memory of a woman to establish her full and fair title to the virtue of chastity. That such was Mrs Fitzherbert's just prerogative, grounded upon the strictest dictates of her conscience, and supported by the principles of her religion, and sanctioned by the decision of her Church, I am bound at all hazards to establish. To this I consider myself pledged, this I owe to the memory of the dead. This I owe to the cause of virtue, truth and religion, and at any personal risk

---

* *Only a limited edition of this book was published in 1856, and Mr Langdale refused to have it reprinted. It has long since been out of print.*

of imputations of what nature soever, or from what quarter soever, this I am prepared, without reserve to undertake.'

By the publication of this book in 1856, Mr Langdale authoritatively informed the world of the fact that a ceremony of marriage had taken place between the Prince of Wales and Mrs Fitzherbert. Mr Langdale, it is true, was unable to publish the documents which Mrs Fitzherbert had expressly deposited at Coutts Bank to prove her marriage, but he gave a list of them and their purport. The fact that he was refused permission to publish these papers only served to whet the public curiosity as to their contents.

As the years wore by repeated applications were made to see the papers which she deposited at Coutts Bank, but the applications were always met with a *non possumus.* As Mrs Fitzherbert had left no clear directions concerning the disposition of these papers after the deaths of the original trustees, the question had in fact become one of some difficulty.

II. FROM SIR SHANE LESLIE:

The Papers then passed into oblivion and there seemed no possibility of their recovery until Mr W H Wilkins, the historian of the House of Hanover, turned his fascinated attention to the romance of George IV and Mrs Fitzherbert. He enlisted the help and interest of Minney Seymour's surviving daughters, Lady Blanche Haygarth and Lady Constance Leslie, to the latter of whom he dedicated his volumes when finished. They lent him the letters which he used and made every effort to obtain him permission to see the Papers.* The third Duke of Wellington was enlisted and kindly wrote to Coutts Bank and reported to Lady Constance that there was no such box held in his name and Lord Albemarle's! This, apparently, because they were not held at the first Duke's disposal.

All enquiries were bound to lead to no result, had it not been that the mystery of the sealed packet had interested a

---

* *In the prelude of Sir Shane Leslie's first book on Mrs Fitzherbert he states that they made information available (to Mr Wilkins) from their archives on condition that 'no caricatures were used and the question of Mrs Fitzherbert's children was to be considered closed.'*

more important personage. King Edward VII of Peacemaking Memory was pleased to pay visits to the House of Keppel of which Lord Albemarle is the head. In answer to a question by the present author the present and eighth Lord Albemarle kindly wrote:

'The Lord Albemarle, you refer to was the Fourth Earl, my great-Grandfather, Master of the Horse to William IV and Queen Victoria. He was an intimate friend of George IV. As you say, Mrs Fitzherbert's private papers were confided to him and placed in Coutts Bank, and when he died they remained there in the custody of my Great Uncle the Hon and Rev Canon Edward Southwell Keppel,* who however left no directions for them to be transferred to the Custody of my Father the Seventh Earl or me.

It was during one of Edward VII's visits to us here that he asked me the very question you now put. My reply was that I had no authority to show them to him, but I did not, as far as I remember, add that I had never seen them.

To this His Majesty made no rejoinder, and the matter ceased to occupy my thoughts.

The next I heard of it was that Lord Knollys made his appearance in Coutts Bank, saying that he had come with instructions from Edward VII to take away Mrs Fitzherbert's papers and that is the last I heard of the matter.'

The King's instructions were not to take away but to examine the Papers and report privately. Mr Wilkins had applied to the King for permission to see the Papers. As he wrote in his Preface to *George IV and Mrs Fitzherbert:*

'These papers were still in existence, and, acting with the approval of the representatives of Mrs Fitzherbert's family and friends, I made an application to His Majesty to see them, at the same time submitting the peculiar circumstances of the case. His Majesty was graciously pleased to grant my request.'

The underlying current was perhaps a little different. **What actually happened was that Mr Wilkins mentioned the Papers to Sir Alfred Fripp, his friend. Fripp was the King's surgeon and passed the suggestion to the late Lady**

** Messrs Coutts wish to point out that they never admitted the Keppel claim to custody of the Papers.*

Warwick, who persuaded the King to make the demand.*

The King sent Lord Knollys as his representative to Coutts Bank. There was no representative of the Fitzherbert family present nor of any of the Executors. Mr Wilkins was permitted to attend and immediately described the scene in a letter to Lady Constance Leslie (February 15, 1905):

'On Friday last I went with Lord Knollys to Coutts and he opened the packet. There were a great many more papers than we expected to find in it and it ended by his sealing the packet up again and taking the papers off to Buckingham Palace. He said he couldn't possibly decide on his own responsibility; the King must see them and he would then let me know. Up till now I have heard nothing further. What there was in the packet that flurried Lord Knollys so much I don't know – he said it couldn't possibly be published.

The certificate of marriage was there, also a letter of George IV to Mrs Fitzherbert forty-four pages long – also a copy of the letter which she wrote to him on his deathbed and a great many more papers of which I know nothing. The list printed in Langdale's book is therefore not correct. I said I would be content if they gave me the marriage certificate, the letter of the clergyman who performed the ceremony and Lord Knollys said he would communicate with me about it. That is all I can tell you and it isn't very satisfactory. I am afraid the King may throw the whole bundle on the fire! There is certainly some mystery which we shall never know – Lord Knollys seemed quite flustered and he is generally so phlegmatic! I have now written the book except for these papers . . . I have told you and Lady Blanche (Haygarth) but no one else about this . . .'

This letter is accurate except that Lord Knollys did not take the Papers to Buckingham Palace. The record offered by Coutts Bank must be regarded as the historic truth. Mr R Brooke-Caws, Curator of the Coutts Museum, has kindly called our attention to an *Envelope marked 're Fitzherbert Papers' containing certain papers relating to the inspection and handing over of the Papers in February, 1905*. From which we are assured that

* *Private information.*

'Lord Knollys called at the Bank on the 10th February, 1905, by desire of the King to inspect the Fitzherbert papers. In Mr W R Malcolm, the Senior Partner's presence the envelope was opened containing them and upon examination it appeared that any decision as to publication must rest with the King.

Before Lord Knollys' visit Mr Malcolm wrote to Mr W J Jarrett on the 6th February, 1905. Mr Jarrett, as surviving Executor of the surviving Executor of Lord Albemarle who survived Lord Stourton, was considered to be the person legally entitled to the papers. He signed a form on the 8th February approving of Coutts & Co's permitting Lord Knollys and Mr W H Wilkins having access to the brown paper parcel containing the papers.

On the 11th February, 1905, Lord Knollys sent a letter saying that the King would like to see the papers. He asked for their delivery to the bearer* from whom a receipt was taken.

On the 13th April Mr W R Malcolm wrote to Lord Knollys to ascertain the King's wishes with regard to the papers, pointing out Coutts & Co's legal position, in view of the fact that the papers had been deposited with them for safe custody.

Lord Knollys in his reply (14th April, 1905) wrote:

"...I was under the impression that you thought the 'legal' possessor of the Fitzherbert Papers would give them to the King. His Majesty read them and directed them to be deposited with other Family Papers of interest at Windsor Castle....

If, however, the 'legal' possessor wishes to have them, they will, of course, be returned to him, but **there can be no doubt that Papers of this description, which only now concern the Sovereign, should be in his possession and not in that of a private individual.**"

Mr W R Malcolm's reply (15th April, 1905) states his approval as follows:

"... My own view is that where the papers are now is far the best place they could be in, and your intimation that, should the person legally entitled to them desire to have them, they

---

* *The bearer was a member of The Life Guards.*

will be returned to him, would be a sufficient reply in the event of a demand being made which I am quite certain will never happen."

Mr W J Jarrett signed a letter (26th April, 1905) signifying his approval of the papers having been handed to the King. Mr F W Stephenson (as executor of his father Sir A K Stephenson, who was executor of Edward Keppel, who was executor of the Earl of Albemarle who deposited the papers) also added his approval.'

His Majesty immediately showed them to his faithful Equerry, Sir Seymour Fortescue, who happened not only to be in attendance on the King, but a grandson of Minney Seymour and to that extent a representative of Mrs Fitz-herbert.

The Papers were not thrown into the fire but deposited in the Archives at Windsor with the following note from Lord Esher:

'These Papers were handed to me by King Edward in April 1905. They were subsequently bound and placed by the King's orders among the Private Archives.'

Subsequently Mr Wilkins published parts of the Prince's Will, that was made in Mrs Fitzherbert's favour and the all-important Marriage Licence by permission of King Edward, through whose chivalrous acceptance of the documents of history Mrs Fitzherbert's character and position were cleared for all time.

In Coutts Bank remains the envelope in which the Fitzherbert papers were contained thus inscribed:

'THE EARL OF ALBEMARLE DECEASED AND LORD STOURTON DECEASED.

Fitzherbert papers.

The Papers contained in this Packet are on NO ACCOUNT to be delivered up without reference to Our Solicitors.

E M(arjoribanks) H L A(ntrobus).

5th May, 1877.

The enclosed packet was opened in my presence by Lord Knollys who attended at 440 Strand for the purpose by command of HM the King.

W R Malcolm
10th February, 1905

Certain papers handed by me to a member of the Life Guards sent from Buckingham Palace, February 11th, 1905.

W R Malcolm

Mr Brooke-Caws notes:
It is interesting to note that the view expressed by Coutts & Co in 1846 (that Lord Albemarle as survivor was entitled to the papers) was that which prevailed in 1905, for, when the papers were given up, steps were apparently not taken to obtain the consent of the representatives of Lord Stourton.'

THE FITZHERBERT PAPERS
1784-1856

preserved at Coutts Bank with sundry additions are as follows in the Archives of Windsor Castle at this day:

1, 2. Memoranda.
3. George, Prince of Wales, to Mrs Fitzherbert.
4. Testimony of Witnesses of Marriage of Mrs Fitzherbert and George, Prince of Wales.
5. Rev. Robert Burt to Prince of Wales.
6. Lord Loughborough to Prince of Wales.
7. Prince of Wales's Will (1796).
8. Prince of Wales to Mrs Fitzherbert. (1799).
9. Mrs Fitzherbert to King George IV. (1830).
10. Mr Samuel Forster to Mrs Fitzherbert.
11. Royal Warrant re Payment of Annuity to Mrs Fitzherbert.
12. Memoranda.
13. Messrs Coutts & Co to Earl of Albemarle.
14. Messrs Coutts & Co to Hon Charles Langdale.
15. Hon Charles Langdale to Messrs Coutts & Co.
16. Memorandum. (Mr William M Coulthurst).*
17. Memorandum. (Mr Edward Marjoribanks).*
18. Prince of Wales to Mrs Fitzherbert (1784).
19. Royal Warrant re Payment of Annuity to Mrs Fitzherbert.

---

* *Partners in Coutts Bank.*

The Packet was endorsed as follows:
(In the hand of the Duke of Wellington.)
'These papers *are placed by**
Mrs Fitzherbert at Messrs Coutts & Co, at the disposal of the Earl of Albemarle and Lord Stourton according to a Memorandum dated the 24th August, 1833

(signed) WELLINGTON.
ALBEMARLE.
STOURTON.

(In the hand of Mr Dickie, Mr Coutts' Clerk.)
Left by Lord Albemarle 24 Aug. 1833.'

The more important documents undoubtedly were those placed by Mrs Fitzherbert under the benignant glance of William IV. According to Lord Stourton the King was moved to tears on reading 'the certificate of her marriage and another interesting and most affecting paper.'

In reviewing Mr Wilkins' book Father Thurston, S J, asked, 'what were these new revelations? Surely long before this William IV, like all the Royal Family, had been quite satisfied that there had been a marriage.'

It only remains to add that King Edward VII on reading the documents was affected in the same manner as William IV. His Majesty was also pleased to send a most kind and gracious message to Mr Wilkins, who was dying at the time.

---

* *The Duke wrote and then erased the words 'belong to'.*

BIBLIOGRAPHY

1) *Memoirs of Mrs Fitzherbert with an account of her marriage with HRH the Prince of Wales* by the Hon Charles Langdale. 1856.
2) *Mrs Fitzherbert & George IV.* 1905. W H Wilkins. Longmans Green.
3) *George IV.* Shane Leslie. 1926. Ernest Benn.
4) *A History of the Royal Pavilion, Brighton.* 1939. Henry D Roberts *(Country Life)*
5) *Mrs Fitzherbert.* Shane Leslie. 1939. Burns, Oates & Washbourne.
6) *Letters of Mrs Fitzherbert.* 1940. Shane Leslie. Burns, Oates & Washbourne.
7) *The Regent and His Daughter.* Dormer Creston. 1943. Eyre & Spottiswoode.
8) *Mrs Fitzherbert.* Anita Leslie. 1960. Hutchinson.
9) *The History of the Althorpe and Pytchley Hunt.* Guy Paget. 1938. William Collins.
10) *Biographies of English Catholics in the Eighteenth Century.* 1909. Rev John Kirk DD. Burns & Oates.
11) *The Prince of Pleasure.* J B Priestley. Heinemann. 1969.
12) *The Life and Times of George IV.* Alan Palmer. 1972. Weidenfeld & Nicolson.
13) *King William IV.* Philip Ziegler. Collins. 1971.

HISTORIES.
1) *History of England.* G M Trevelyan.
2) *English Social History.* G M Trevelyan.
3) *The Age of Elegance.* Arthur Bryant.
4) *The Oxford Illustrated History of Britain.* Editor Kenneth O Morgan.
5) *Historical Atlas of Britain.* Editors Falkus and Gillingham.

6) *The Concise Encyclopaedia of World History*. Editor John Bowle.

ANNOTATIONS/SOURCES

This book is based on documentary information which can be annotated, current research, and the knowledge that has passed down through the five generations of descendants, to those alive today.

1. Lord Albemarle's Memoirs, Mary Frampton's Diary & Lady Constance Leslie.
2. Lord Colchester's Diaries.
3. Short biography of Thomas Fitzherbert of Swynnerton. From 'Biographies of English Catholics in the Eighteenth Century' by Rev John Kirk D.D., and the Fitzherbert Family.
4. Lady Horatia's mother, born Maria Walpole, whose first husband was Lord Waldegrave, was the illegitimate daughter of Sir Edward Walpole and Mary Clement, a milliner's apprentice. Lady Waldegrave later married secretly the Duke of Gloucester, brother of George III. It was this clandestine marriage and that of his brother, the Duke of Cumberland, which inspired the Royal Marriage Act of 1772.
5. 'I am informed on trustworthy authority that it (Gifford Lodge) was the private residence of Mrs Fitzherbert and her children, Marble Hill being the house wherein guests were entertained.' Mrs Fitzherbert by Shane Leslie. Page 16.
6. Parish Records. St Thomas, Southwark.
7. Lady Eleanor Butler letter. 18 June 1789.
8. Northamptonshire Record Office.
9. Prince's Will dated 10 January 1796. Fitzherbert papers.
10. Duke of Clarence speaking in the House of Lords and

Pitt's proposals.

11. Mrs Fitzherbert's autobiography dictated to Lord Stourton. Langdale. 1856.
12. History of St Mary's Church, Welford. Geoffrey Pitcher.
13. Will of René Payne. Died 1799.
14. Letter from Sir Harry Englefield to Miss Berry. 18 February 1803.
15. Letter. Lord Euston to Admiral Payne. Ragley papers.
16. Parliamentary Paper entitled: 'House of Lords. Between Mary Georgiana Emma Seymour, an infant, by William Bentinck, Esquire, her next friend. Appellant The Right Honourable George Fitzroy, commonly called the Earl of Euston, and the Hon Henry Seymour, commonly called Lord Henry Seymour, Respondents.'
17. Northampton Library.
18. History of St Peter's Church, Berkhamsted, Herts.
19. W H Wilkins. Page 2. Also portrait of Walter Smythe and Acton Burnell.
20. W H Wilkins. Page 256.
21. Parish Records. St Luke's Church, Chelsea.
22. Parish Records. St Paul's, Covent Garden.
23. Letter. Mrs Fitzherbert to Minney. 13 September 1824.
24. W H Wilkins. Page 338.
25. Eton College records.
26. Theatre-un-Royal. L Warwick. Northampton Library.
27. Members Memorials of Brook's Club.
28. Letters. Mrs Fitzherbert to Minney from Tunbridge Wells. 13 September 1824. Mrs Fitzherbert to Minney from Chatsworth. 17 October 1825.
29. Letter. Mrs Fitzherbert to Minney. 1825.
30. History of the Althorpe and Pytchley Hunt. Guy Paget.
31. Dictionary of National Biography.
32. The Royal Pavilion, Brighton by Henry D Roberts.
33. Payne papers.
34. In 1830 George Payne enlarged Sulby Hall considerably. Northampton Record Office.
35. Sir William Knighton's Diary and Memoirs of Sir Wm Knighton.

36. W H Wilkins. Page 371. Letters of Mrs Fitzherbert. Shane Leslie. Page 54.
37. Earl of Albemarle to Lord Stourton. 25 August 1833.
38. Letter. Mrs Fitzherbert to Minney. 26 December 1835.
39. Kensington Rate Books.
40. Pigot's Directory.
41. PO Directory.
42. Letter. Royal Archives. (RA HH1 - 223).
43. Joseph Foster's Alumni Oxonienses and Crockford's Clerical Directory.
44. A Landmark in Brighton. St Paul's Church. Ben Surrey. The Sussex County Magazine.
45. Letter. Royal Archives. (PPadd Vic. 1104(1859)) and Brighton Census 1861.
46. Payne papers.
47. Title Deeds of Heath House.
48. Mrs Fitzherbert by Shane Leslie. Prelude xi: confirmed by Payne family knowledge.
49. Mrs Fitzherbert by Anita Leslie. '. . . she destroyed all reference to Mrs Fitzherbert's issue.'
50. Sir John Soane's Museum records.

LIST OF ILLUSTRATIONS